# BADLANDS
## THEODORE ROOSEVELT AND WIND CAVE

### NATIONAL PARKS

By Michael Milstein
Photography by Michael H. Francis

NORTHWORD

NORTHWORD PRESS, INC.
Minocqua, Wisconsin

For Robert Sherrill, who showed me the fun in writing.

## ACKNOWLEDGMENTS

Thanks to all those who took time to review the manuscript and suggest improvements, particularly Marianne Mills at Badlands National Park, Ron Terry at Wind Cave National Park, Bruce Kaye at Theodore Roosevelt National Park and Barbara Harold at NorthWord Press. Photographer Michael Francis deserves high praise for capturing so many marvelous creatures on film. Thanks also to those who had the foresight to protect these special national parks and those who continue to protect them, now and for the future. Finally, thanks to my best and favorite critic: my wife, Susan.

© Michael Milstein, 1996
Photography © Michael H. Francis, 1996
Additional Photography © 1996: LuRay Parker, 41; C. Allan Morgan, 58, 61; Tom Vezo/The Wildlife Collection, 71; Gary Meszaros/Dembinsky Photo Associates, 93.

Cover design by Lisa Moore
Book design by Kenneth Hey

NorthWord Press, Inc.
P.O. Box 1360
Minocqua, WI 54548

For a free catalog describing our audio products, nature books and calendars, call **1-800-356-4465**, or write Consumer Inquiries, NorthWord Press, Inc., P.O. Box 1360, Minocqua, Wisconsin 54548.

Library of Congress Cataloging-in-Publication Data

Milstein, Michael.
    Badlands, Teddy Roosevelt & Wind Cave National Parks : a wildlife watcher's guide / by Michael Milstein : Michael H. Francis, photographer.
        p.    cm.
    Includes bibliographical references.
    ISBN 1-55971-575-8  (sc)
    1. Wildlife watching—South Dakota—Badlands National Park—Guidebooks.    2. Wildlife watching—North Dakota—Theodore Roosevelt National Park—Guidebooks.    3. Wildlife watching—South Dakota—Wind Cave National Park—Guidebooks.    4. Wildlife viewing sites—South Dakota—Badlands National Park—Guidebooks.    5. Wildlife viewing sites—North Dakota—Theodore Roosevelt National Park—Guidebooks.    6. Wildlife viewing sites—South Dakota—Wind Cave National Park—Guidebooks.    7. Badlands National Park (S.D.)—Guidebooks.    8. Theodore Roosevelt National Park (N.D.)—Guidebooks.    9. Wind Cave National Park (S.D.)—Guidebooks.    I. Title

    Ql205.M55  1996
    599.09783—dc20                                        96-11587

Printed in Hong Kong

# Contents

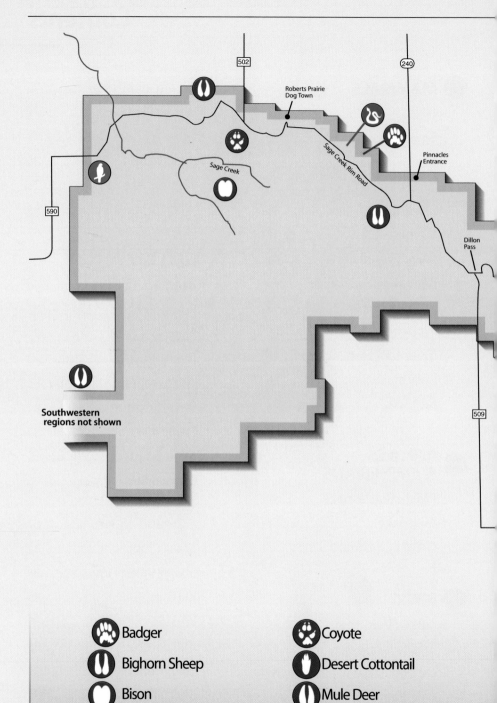

Southwestern
regions not shown

Roberts Prairie
Dog Town

Sage Creek

Sage Creek Rim Road

Pinnacles
Entrance

Dillon
Pass

502

240

590

509

Badger

Bighorn Sheep

Bison

Black-tailed Prairie Dog

Coyote

Desert Cottontail

Mule Deer

Prairie Rattlesnake

# Badlands National Park

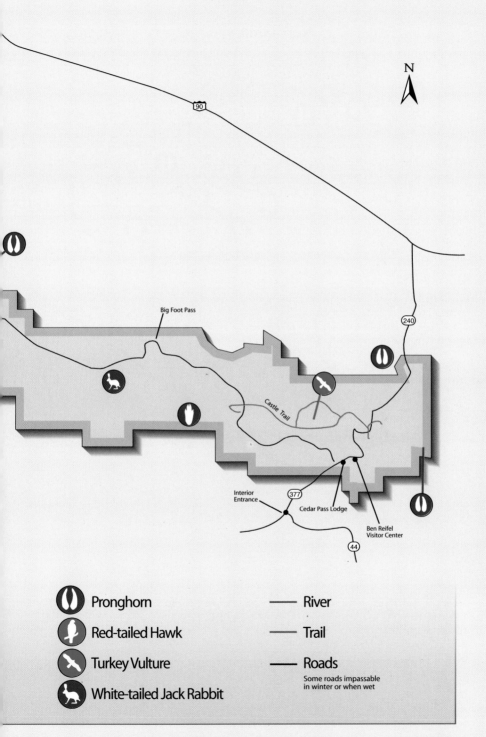

# North Unit

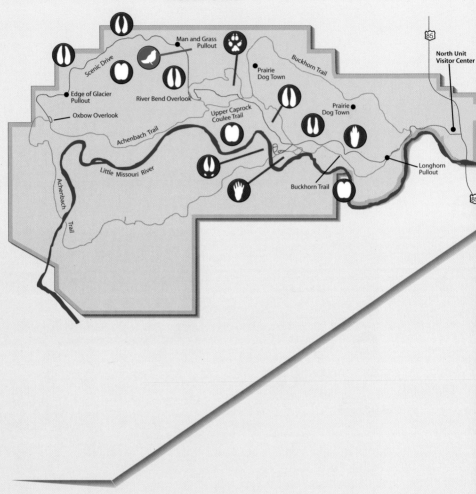

## Legend

 Badger

 Beaver

 Bighorn Sheep

 Bison

 Black-tailed Prairie Dog

 Bobcat

 Coyote

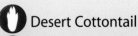 Desert Cottontail

 Elk

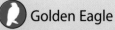 Golden Eagle

 Mule Deer

# Theodore Roosevelt National Park

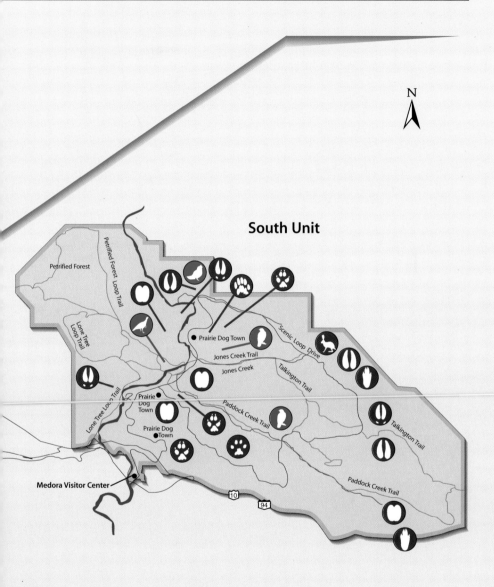

N

**South Unit**

Petrified Forest

Petrified Forest Loop Trail

Lone Tree Loop Trail

Prairie Dog Town

Scenic Loop Drive

Jones Creek Trail

Jones Creek

Talkington Trail

Lone Tree Loop Trail

Prairie Dog Town

Paddock Creek Trail

Prairie Dog Town

Talkington Trail

Medora Visitor Center

Paddock Creek Trail

10

94

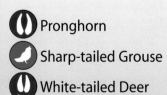

Pronghorn

Sharp-tailed Grouse

White-tailed Deer

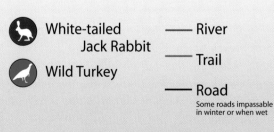

White-tailed
Jack Rabbit

Wild Turkey

—— River

—— Trail

—— Road
Some roads impassable
in winter or when wet

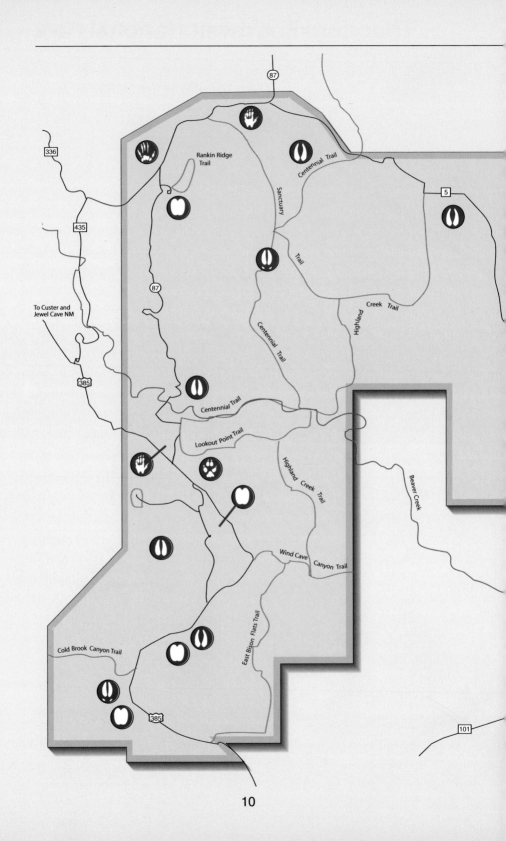

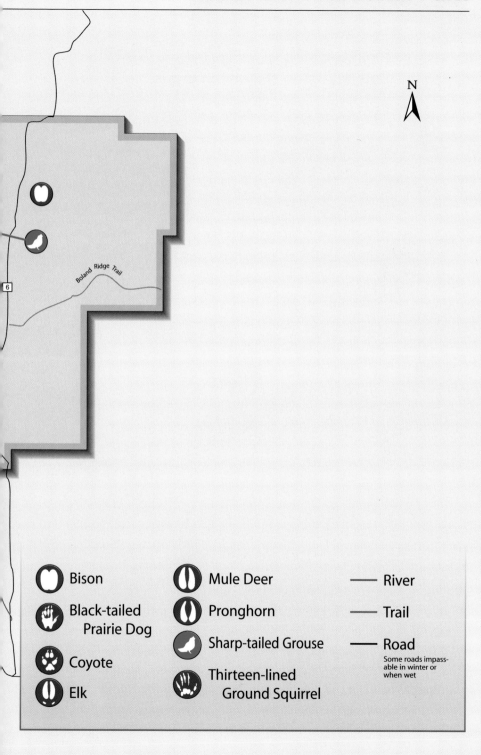

N

Boland Ridge Trail

6

| | | |
|---|---|---|
| Bison | Mule Deer | —— River |
| Black-tailed Prairie Dog | Pronghorn | —— Trail |
| Coyote | Sharp-tailed Grouse | —— Road |
| Elk | Thirteen-lined Ground Squirrel | Some roads impassable in winter or when wet |

# INTRODUCTION

Wildlife was not the reason for the creation of Badlands, Wind Cave or Theodore Roosevelt national parks. At first a national monument, Badlands was established in 1939 to protect the fossils of wild animals

that roamed the region millions of years before. Wind Cave was set aside in 1903 to protect the web of gloriously decorated passages that twist through the earth hundreds of feet below the surface.

Theodore Roosevelt National Park was established in 1947 to preserve the historic haunts of the nation's twenty-sixth president. While Theodore Roosevelt had clearly enjoyed observing and hunting the wild animals that ranged there, the former president had a much higher profile than any of the denizens of the North Dakota wilds. Still, it was the lessons he learned among those vibrant wilds, their pastel sunset colors, chilling winds and the way they echoed the howl of wolves that reinforced Roosevelt's reputation as one of the greatest conservationists in American history. Perhaps they will do the same for you.

## Pieces of the Past

As the West was settled, national parks became refuges for the wildlife that once had the mountains and plains largely to themselves. What was once a great expanse of rich grasslands, a luscious salad bar for the animals that depended on it, was eventually trimmed by human settlement and development to but one percent of its original range. The parks turned into pristine slices of this immense prairie of the past, places where herds of elk, pronghorn antelope and bison still dominate the landscape. Of all the species native to the parks, only the wolf and grizzly bear remain absent. Today, a visit to Badlands, Wind Cave or Theodore Roosevelt national parks holds unprecedented promise as an American wildlife safari of the first order, where sightings of the most prominent wild creatures on the continent are not only likely, but are also, if you look in the right spot, virtually guaranteed.

This book should help make the most of your expedition. It is not an exhaustive summary of every species in the region; instead, it's a friendly guide that will lead you on a tour of discovery through the impressive trio of national parks that adorn the western sections of North and South Dakota. You'll step beyond the obvious attractions of each park to find a wealth of wildlife that is just as intriguing. You'll find out how and where to look for animals as diverse the beaver, nature's own engineer, and the black-footed ferret, the rarest mammal in North America and one of the rarest in the world. You'll learn a bit about the animals themselves—how coyotes rely on cunning teamwork to bring down prey and how bats offer the most effective means of insect control anywhere. All you need to do in exchange is to keep your eyes, ears and mind open. If you are willing to find something new, you most assuredly will.

## Native Lands, Native Peoples

Climate influences the landscape. The region is now generally arid, but with enough moisture to nourish grasses that feed many species of wildlife. You may notice differences between the mixtures of vegetation depending on terrain: river plains boast arching cottonwood trees while drier hillsides hold little more than sagebrush, cactus and spring wildflowers. These contrasts are equally apparent to wildlife that depends on the landscape for sustenance through dry summers and icy winters.

People have inhabited the region for more than 12,000 years. The first Native American residents followed favorable climates and hunted mammoths along the way. After a long drought extinguished mammoths and other Ice Age species, new peoples arrived and made their living by hunting bison and small game species and seeking edible roots and berries. Some descendants of the early inhabitants now live on reservations in the region and have interest in the national parks. Part of Badlands National Park is managed jointly with the Oglala Sioux tribe. When park rangers round up bison in both Badlands and Theodore Roosevelt parks to keep the park herds from outstripping their food supply, the surplus animals go to tribes on nearby reservations. The tribes let some of the animals run free, while they kill others for food and materials, using the fur, horns and other parts in sacred ceremonies, as did their ancestors.

National parks are not the only place to find wildlife. As you drive to and between the parks covered in this book, you may pass through the Black Hills National Forest and a variety of national grasslands. These lands are managed differently than national parks: consumptive uses, such as livestock grazing, oil drilling and logging are permitted. But they still harbor plenty of wildlife. Also remember other natural features such as Custer State Park, bordering Wind Cave National Park; Jewel Cave National Monument in the Black Hills; and Devils Tower National Monument just over the state line in Wyoming.

Each holds wildlife; it's just a matter of watching for it.

# WILDLIFE WATCHER'S CODE OF CONDUCT

While peering into the wild realm, take care not to disturb it. Respect for wildlife will reward you and those that come after you with more plentiful wildlife sightings. It will also reward wildlife with the peace and freedom to carry on at their own pace. A few guidelines:

## Don't Feed the Animals

Wildlife that learn to take food from people are no longer wild. Those that learn to connect people with food, whether in the form of handouts or trash, may grow aggressive and dangerous and may eventually have to be killed. Others that come to rely on human handouts starve during the winter.

## Watch from a Distance

Don't get too close. Many animals instinctively defend themselves and their young from intruders, so do not intrude on them. Bison may charge people who get too near. Despite their lumbering look, they can move blindingly fast. Never approach within 100 yards of bison. As long as you watch from a distance and avoid surprising wildlife, you will protect both yourself and the animals.

## Do Not Touch

Watch where you reach. Rattlesnakes, scorpions and spiders may escape summertime heat by hiding under rocks, amid downed trees and in other nooks and crannies. They want as little to do with you as you do with them. Stay alert and do not reach where you cannot see.

## Walk on the Paths

Stay on trails where provided. If a trail leads where you want to go, follow it. Take a good map and compass if hiking in an unfamiliar spot. Pioneering new trails damages vegetation and may lead to erosion.

## Leave Pets at Home

National parks are set aside to protect wild ecosystems of which pets are not a part. Barking dogs may startle and stress wildlife even if they do not mean to. If you do bring pets, keep them leashed and under control. Pets are not allowed either on trails or in the backcountry.

## Drive Carefully

Slow and careful driving may lead to more wildlife observations. The top non-natural cause of death of park wildlife is automobile collisions. Stay on roads, but do not stop on roadways or pull off, except at established overlooks. Remember that wildlife roams free and watch out, especially at night.

## Bring Your Camera

Take only pictures. All natural components of national parks, living or not, are protected. Avoid the urge to collect rocks, bones, fossils or antlers. Leave them for others to see and enjoy.

That said, there's only one more rule: Have fun!

# TIPS FOR WILDLIFE WATCHERS

Watching wildlife is a pleasant pursuit. It takes you outside and introduces you to a fascinating, wild world. Because it is different, though, it's especially important to think ahead and employ common sense when you head into the field. Stop first at visitor centers and look over a map of the spot you are visiting. Ask rangers about weather, road and wildlife viewing conditions; the abundance and visibility of certain species often varies depending on the season and climate. Ranger-led hikes in the summer provide personal introductions to the parks.

Certain vantage points give you an advantage. The short nature trail to a fire lookout at Rankin Ridge in Wind Cave National Park provides a spectacular view of open and tree-studded grasslands. It's a great place to sight elk, bison, pronghorn antelope and other wildlife from a distance. At Badlands National Park, numerous overlooks along the scenic road traversing the North Unit of the park are good spots to watch for wild creatures, since you can look south into a wilderness region where no cars are allowed. Overlooks in Theodore Roosevelt National Park may also expose wildlife. Look for animals along the Little Missouri River, where they quench their thirst, and which nourishes a lush wetland environment all its own.

## In the Field

Think about how to make the most of your visit. While you can cover plenty of territory by car, stepping out for short hikes along trails or to scenic overlooks will expose you to the texture and feel of the land. A half-mile hike along the Ridgeline Nature Trail in the South Unit of Theodore Roosevelt National Park is a good place to start. Stop, look and listen for the forms of life all around you, but watch out for the poison ivy that lines the trail and stay alert for rattlesnakes.

Sounds and movements may lead you to wildlife sightings you might have missed otherwise. Keep watch for dark or light spots on the horizon that might turn out, on closer look, to be bison or elk.

Think about the animals that make their living off the land beneath your feet.

Before you set out, though, make sure you are prepared: wear sturdy shoes, take water and any clothing you will need in case a sudden change in the weather beats you back to the trailhead.

Take along a pair of binoculars, a spotting scope or a telephoto lens for your camera. They will give you a close-up look at wildlife without getting too close.

While it helps to get out from behind the windshield, sometimes your car gives you an advantage. Animals get used to vehicle traffic along roads and may not be bothered if you slow for a look from inside your mobile blind.

Pay attention to sights and sounds. Animals often blend into their surroundings to elude predators and may try to hide from your approach unless you keep still and quiet. You may notice, for instance, the squeak of tree branches is actually the voice of a songbird.

Early morning and late afternoon are usually the best times to find wildlife, for animals, like us, often rest during the glaring heat of midday. Where you look will also influence what you'll see. By examining the entries in this book, for example, you'll find that to locate beavers, you should look for the relaxed tree-lined rivers and streams where they make their homes, while busybody prairie dogs make their presence known by stripping grass down to the ground and dotting their expansive colonies with mounds of dirt that mark the entrances to their burrows.

# WILDLIFE OF THE DARK

Gazing over the undulating, tree-studded grasslands of Wind Cave National Park, it's easy to begin imagining the subterranean web of passageways running beneath them. Walking, crawling, climbing, and even swimming, explorers have found their way through miles and miles of these dark tunnels that were slowly carved by water and time—millions of years of it. More than a century since the telltale exhalation of air that gives Wind Cave its name led to its discovery, the same natural breaths suggest that 95 percent of the cave passageways remain unseen, a world of perpetual blackness. It is a place where light, which serves as the foundation of life on the surface, is entirely unknown.

This would seem to make it an unattractive place to set up house. But in an example of the resoluteness of life itself, a small fraternity of wild creatures does make its home in the deep, dark, dank reaches of this underworld.

Of all the animals that live in caves, probably the best known is the bat. Although not full-time cave-dwellers, bats utilize caves and mines as protected roosting sites between their nighttime flights in search of food and as places to hibernate through the winter.

Oddly, though, few bats make their home in Wind Cave. No one is quite sure why. It may be that the constant breezes blowing in or out of the Cave to balance the Cave's barometric pressure with that of the outside air interferes with their flight patterns, as wind does with airplanes. It may also have something to do with the temperature of the Cave. The interior temperatures of most caves equal the average annual temperature outside, but heat from deep within the Earth appears to keep Wind Cave several degrees warmer than the outside average. The warmer temperature may keep hibernating bats from lowering their body metabolism enough to survive the winter on nothing but their fat stores. A few bats have been found hibernating in Wind Cave, but all ended up dying before winter was over.

By contrast, the lengthy labyrinth protected within nearby Jewel Cave National Monument is popular with bats. Thousands of bats representing seven or more species often roost and hibernate in Jewel Cave; the National Park Service puts the Cave's natural entrance off-limits to visitors during the winter so as not to disturb the sleeping flyers. Bats may frighten some people, but they are valuable, especially if you're not crazy about mosquitoes and their insect brethren. Bats eat bugs. The bat population of Jewel Cave may gobble a million or more insects in one summer night.

Cave rats, also known as wood rats, have occasionally roamed Wind Cave, feeling their way with long whiskers and leaving scent trails so they can retrace their routes back out of the dark.

Little else is known about the residents of Wind Cave, but a 1959 survey found several insect species that are partial to caves and probably feed on organic matter seeping into the Cave with water from the surface. One was a cave cricket, wielding long antennae to help find its way through cave passages in the dark. Others were tiny insects called "springtails," which are about the size of small ants. At least one variety of springtail found in Wind Cave appeared to be a species never detected anywhere else. Other such species may exist in the perpetual blackness of the underground—it's just that no one has discovered them yet.

# THUNDERING HERDS

Most national parks pay tribute to native ecosystems, to environments as they existed before human hands began manipulating the scenery. But the existence of Theodore Roosevelt National Park is due not only to the extraordinary natural scene of the North Dakota badlands, but also to the region's historic link with a president who is also remembered as a great conservationist. In pursuit of that goal, park managers maintain controlled populations of wild horses and longhorn cattle, both non-native to the area but historically important animals that were prominent during Theodore Roosevelt's time.

## Wild Horses

There are few images as inherently western as a band of mustangs thundering through sagebrush, dust billowing in their wake. But the wild horse is, strangely, both an ancient and recent color in the palette of the West.

Horses lived in the wilds of North America through the ages. But by the end of what is known as the Pleistocene epoch around 10,000 years ago, they had become extinct, living on only in Europe and Asia. When Spanish voyagers began scouting the New World, they brought horses with them—the horses fostered exploration and settlement that might have been nearly impossible otherwise. Through the years, though, some horses invariably escaped and reverted to the wild, where they were called mustangs, a derivative of the Spanish word *"mesteno,"* which means wild. Native Americans who had lived in a hunter-gatherer economy quickly learned the value of the horse for hunting buffalo and for waging war; probably no other single development, besides the arrival of Europeans from the Old World, so greatly affected the ways of American Indian tribes.

From then on, horses were a critical element of the West. Their wild versions, Theodore Roosevelt wrote, were doubtless of domestic origin, "being either themselves runaways from some ranch or Indian outfit, or else claiming such for their sires and dams, yet are quite as wild as the antelope on whose domain they have intruded."

The unregulated ramblings of wild horse herds earned the disdain of ranchers who wanted grazing lands for their livestock; many horse herds were eliminated during the early 1900s. North Dakota cowboys would also corral wild horses and turn them into domestic stock. But then horse advocates began demanding the preservation of at least some relic populations of the wild mustangs and the government slowly integrated that demand into its wildlife policies. Even in Theodore Roosevelt National Park, the National Park Service tried to eliminate wild horses from the park because they were a non-native species. But by 1970, park managers had come to see horses as an element of the park's historic value and decided to let some mustangs remain. The park staff now allows a free-ranging horse herd (within the park—the park boundary is fenced) of about 50 to 90 horses. Periodic roundups keep horse numbers within those thresholds; excess horses are sold at auction. Even with such intensive manage-ment, the park's mustang population has apparently maintained its wild lineage, for the unusual white "apron" color patterns that adorn many of the animals resemble those of nineteenth century horses that are rarely seen among domestic horses today.

In their wild state, park mustangs behave like other wild animals, grouping into bands of between five and fifteen horses, led by a stallion and including several mares that are his mates and their offspring. As the colts grow older, they may find themselves kicked out of their original band to form one of their own. Bands claim their own territories, with the lead stallions defending their territories and their mares from intrusions.

Look for wild horses in the southeast section of the national park's South Unit and along the park boundary where it parallels Interstate 94. The Painted Canyon Overlook and Buck Hill are good places to scan the terrain for bands of horses. But if you spot any, watch them through binoculars and keep your distance. Wild horses are wary, easily disturbed and very strong and fast; you do not want to be in their way.

An odd equine relative is easily spotted in Custer State Park, adja-cent to Wind Cave National Park in South Dakota's Black Hills. That is the burro, first imported from New Mexico to carry tourists up Harney Peak. A limited number of burros now wander free along the park's wildlife loop.

## Longhorns

Another domestic animal whose history is intertwined with that of the West is the Texas longhorn. As bison disappeared from the Great Plains in the wake of the non-stop machine of civilization, ranchers began importing longhorns to take the place of the great buffalo herds. The North Dakota grasslands and badlands seemed perfect, Theodore Roosevelt wrote, his opinion built on the statements of more experienced cattlemen: "We have questioned many of them and the invariable answer has been that nowhere in the United States is there a better cattle country than the Bad Lands."

There followed a kind of gold rush of the cattle industry as cattle drives rivaling the masses of bison they replaced pushed thousands upon thousands of longhorns into the Dakotas. The North Dakota Badlands cattle boom took off in the summer of 1883, when some 50,000 cattle arrived and began chomping the green and tender grasses and when Roosevelt took his first look at the region's surreal shapes of earth and sky. It was his investments in cattle and ranch-lands that brought him back to the Badlands in succeeding years, when his herds and his favor for the country grew. Land and grass were virtually free for the taking, but handling cattle required work.

In the winter of 1886-87, the cattle boom went bust. Roosevelt saw that ballooning numbers of cattle were wearing out the range, already frayed by a severe drought. Then blinding snowstorms and weeks of bone-chilling cold devastated the herds, killing more cattle than even the most pessimistic ranchers could have expected. That was the end of Roosevelt's cowboy days: he returned to the West now and then, but never with the same vigor.

An element of the brief glory days of the cattle boom lives on in the North Unit of Theodore Roosevelt National Park with a small herd of Texas longhorn cattle. Longhorns are uncommon in ranching opera-tions today, but park managers have seen fit to keep some on so visitors can find a more complete historical picture of the land. Watch for the one-of-a-kind shape of the longhorn, with dual horns that curve around like giant fishhooks and may measure nine feet from one end to the other, a few miles after entering the North Unit. The Longhorn Pullout offers a good vantage point that is most productive early or late in the day, since the cattle seek shade from the hot midday sun.

# WILDLIFE ENCOUNTERS

■ Common  ◧ Occasional  □ Rare  — None

| | Badlands | Wind Cave* | Theodore Roosevelt |
|---|---|---|---|
| **MAMMALS** | | | |
| Beaver | □ | □ | ◧ |
| Bighorn Sheep | ■ | □ | ◧ |
| Bison | ■ | ■ | ■ |
| Black-footed Ferret | □ | — | — |
| Black-tailed Prairie Dog | ■ | ■ | ■ |
| Bobcat | □ | □ | ◧ |
| Coyote | ◧ | ◧ | ◧ |
| Elk | — | ■ | ■ |
| Mountain Lion | □ | □ | □ |
| Mule Deer | ■ | ■ | ■ |
| Pronghorn | ■ | ■ | ■ |
| Red Fox | □ | □ | □ |
| White-tailed Deer | ◧ | ■ | ■ |
| **REPTILES/ AMPHIBIANS** | | | |
| Bullsnake | ◧ | ■ | ◧ |
| Great Plains Toad | ◧ | ◧ | ◧ |
| Prairie Rattlesnake | ■ | ◧ | ◧ |
| **BIRDS** | | | |
| American Kestrel | ◧ | □ | ◧ |
| Bald Eagle | □ | □ | ◧ |
| Black-billed Magpie | ■ | ■ | ■ |
| Red-shafted Flicker | ■ | ■ | ■ |
| Golden Eagle | ◧ | ◧ | ◧ |
| Great Horned Owl | ◧ | ◧ | ■ |
| Horned Lark | ◧ | ◧ | ◧ |
| Mountain Bluebird | ◧ | ■ | ◧ |
| Red-tailed Hawk | ■ | ■ | ■ |
| Turkey Vulture | ■ | ◧ | ■ |
| Western Meadowlark | ◧ | ■ | ■ |
| Wild Turkey | □ | ■ | ■ |
| **GALLERY** | | | |
| Badger | ◧ | ◧ | ◧ |
| Cliff Swallow | ■ | ■ | ■ |
| Common Crow | ■ | ■ | ■ |
| Common Nighthawk | ◧ | ■ | ◧ |
| Deer Mouse | ■ | ■ | ■ |
| Desert Cottontail | ■ | ■ | ■ |
| Killdeer | ◧ | ◧ | ◧ |
| Least Chipmunk | ■ | ■ | ■ |
| Long-tailed Weasel | □ | □ | □ |
| Mink | — | — | ◧ |
| Northern Shrike | ◧ | ◧ | ◧ |
| Porcupine | ■ | ■ | ■ |
| Raccoon | ◧ | ◧ | ◧ |
| Sandhill Crane | □ | □ | ◧ |
| Sharp-tailed Grouse | ◧ | ■ | ◧ |
| Striped Skunk | ◧ | ◧ | ◧ |
| Thirteen-lined Ground Squirrel | ■ | ■ | ◧ |
| Western Kingbird | ◧ | ◧ | ◧ |
| White-tailed Jack Rabbit | ◧ | ◧ | ◧ |

* Listings for Wind Cave National Park also reflect wildlife-viewing opportunities in adjacent Custer State Park.

# MAMMALS

## ELK

When Theodore Roosevelt established his second ranch in the weather-worn North Dakota badlands, now part of the national park that bears his name, he called it the Elkhorn. And with good reason. Elk *(Cervus elaphus)*, also known by the Native American given name of wapiti (a Shawnee Indian term for "white rump"), are one of the most majestic of all native species of wildlife. Beyond the rich, brown coats and distinguished manes worn by males stand their spectacular antlers, scraping the sky like a pair of massive swords that surpass a human's reach.

Elk were once the most widespread of all hoofed animals in North America, their range blanketing nearly the entire continent. Human settlement gradually pushed them westward and heavy hunting pressure eventually eliminated the regal creatures even in much of the West. To restore the original cast of wildlife, managers of Wind Cave and Theodore Roosevelt national parks imported elk and released them within the parks, where the initial animals have given rise to healthy populations. Today Wind Cave boasts a herd of about 300 elk, with another 300 or so in residence at the South Unit of Theodore Roosevelt. Occasional roundups keep elk numbers in line with their range. Grasslands in and around what is now Badlands National Park also held elk, which became the targets of market hunters providing meat for the gold camps of the nearby Black Hills. No elk roam Badlands today.

Look for elk foraging in the early morning and late afternoon at the forest's edge. They are part of the deer family, but far exceed their relatives in size. Large bulls may weigh more than 1,000 pounds and stand nearly 10 feet high, excluding their antlers, which may extend another five feet or more and usually bear a dozen tines (six on each side) when mature. Only males carry antlers, which fall off in spring and sprout again, growing as much as a half-inch per day during the summer when they bear a velvety surface rich in blood. As fall approaches, bulls rub their racks against trees to polish and sharpen them in preparation for courtship clashes, where they ram their antlers together in a natural drama that determines dominance and, more importantly, access to females. The "rut," as the mating season is called, is a high point in the lives of elk and is marked by the wailing bugles of males intent on gathering harems of females, or cows, with which they will breed. There are tales of bull elk entangling their antlers during bitter face-offs and dying that way.

Cow elk typically leave their herds in late spring and give birth to young in secluded spots where they can guard for predators. Adult elk aggressively defend their young. Summer draws elk to the cooler high country, but they will migrate back toward familiar winter range come fall. Elk carry a golden brown coat that serves as camouflage amid the feathery grasses of summer, but their telltale white rumps may give them away. Both males and females are adept swimmers and may run up to 35 miles per hour, dodging trees and brush so sprightly they move in near silence.

## Where To Find Elk

At Wind Cave National Park, elk are commonly seen from the park road south of the visitor center, from overlooks in the northern uplands and in adjacent Custer State Park. At Theodore Roosevelt National Park, watch for elk from viewpoints in the South Unit.

## BISON

American Indians and early pioneers who set out to colonize the West witnessed a wildlife spectacle that seems almost unimaginable today. They saw streams, rivers, even torrents of deep brown fur that darkened the prairie for miles—sometimes as far as the eye could see. The fur belonged to bison *(Bison bison)*, also called buffalo (derived from the French term for oxen), that once was the paramount species on the prairies of the West. It is the largest land mammal in North America and, at one time, was one of the most numerous, with a population that approached 60 million or more.

Weighing in at nearly a ton, large bull bison have the heft of small automobiles and can move nearly as fast, belying their often lumbering appearance. Keep your distance. Bison roam with single-minded devotion: head down, grazing, shaggy mane, horns pointed straight up. Nothing much stands in their way. In winter, they use their broad head like a bulldozer, plowing snow so they can reach the vegetarian meal that lies underneath. They are most active early and late in the day and tend to travel in separate male and female herds except during mating season. But lone bison are numerous, too. It is their numbers that give them such strength: western settlers described adult bison encircling their calves in a kind of living fortress designed to deter marauding wolves.

Native Indian tribes relied on bison for the staples of their existence: meat to eat, fur to fend off the cold, horns and teeth for sacred ceremonies. Archaeologists have found jumbled bison bones adjacent to the Ancient Hunters Overlook near the Pinnacles entrance to Badlands National Park; they suspect that American Indian hunters drove herds of the animals up a gulch leading to a steep cliff that became a buffalo jump. After the bulky creatures tumbled over the precipice to their deaths, the Indians would butcher the carcasses and collect their necessities in the process.

During the second half of the 1800s, as the human population of the West grew, American bison were slaughtered with abandon, mostly for their meat (mainly tongues) and luxurious hides, other times simply for sport, if you could call it that. By the turn of the century, fewer than 1,000 bison were left and the massive herds that once colored the prairie were only a memory. In 1913, the National Park Service restored a bit of that memory by freeing 14 bison donated by the Bronx Zoo in Wind Cave National Park and, later, by resurrecting additional herds in Badlands and Theodore Roosevelt national parks, where they have flourished. It is now common in summer to see bison foraging and rolling in dust wallows—often in prairie dog towns—to shake annoying insects. Mating begins in late summer and features head-smashing contests between males; reddish calves are born the following spring. Winter prompts bison to grow shaggier coats which peel off in chunks when the weather moderates.

## Where To Find Bison

There's a reason Bison Flats in the southern end of Wind Cave National Park bears that name—watch for the shaggy silhouettes amid swaying grass on both sides of the road. At Badlands National Park, bison stay in the Sage Creek Basin, visible from overlooks and the Sage Creek Rim Road. Bison roam both the North and South Units of Theodore Roosevelt National Park; watch for them especially along creek bottoms and within prairie dog towns, where vigorous regrowth of grasses offers bountiful meals. Whatever you do, do not approach these massive creatures.

## MULE DEER

If you have seen mules and you see mule deer *(Odocoileus hemionus)*, you will know instantly how the abundant grazers got their name. Their big mule-like ears, each one nearly as large as their entire head, move separately and almost constantly. They efficiently home in on any sound that might betray an approaching mountain lion, coyote or other hazards. If they do detect danger, mulies bounce away in giant four-legged leaps stretching up to 20 feet, a gait that makes them look like living pogo sticks.

Mule deer are abundant, frequenting both forest stands and open prairie, and sometimes traveling many miles in their ongoing search for food. They also migrate from high to low elevations along with the

32

seasons. Mule deer turn from bronze-red in summer to gray and dark brown during other times of the year and are set off by a light-colored rump. Bucks grow antlers annually. The left and right branches of their racks are normally mirror images, with several tines that split in two, like the arms of a tree. Buck mule deer face off to win over does; usually the buck with the largest antlers triumphs. Does give birth to twin, spotted fawns in the summer. Newborn fawns usually have no distinguishing odor, which effectively protects them from predators that follow their noses.

Watch for evidence of deer dining as you walk through the parks. Because they lack sharp upper teeth, deer tear off vegetation rather than clipping it cleanly like rabbits or other species. Leafy plants supply deer with most of their food, but their voracious appetites also lead them to alternate dishes including blackberries and huckleberries, fir twigs, cedar, aspen, willow dogwood and even that western standby, sagebrush.

## Where To Find Mule Deer

Mule deer can be found just about anywhere in all of the three national parks. Look especially in fields in late afternoon and on roadsides, where tender vegetation is a lure. Be careful driving at night: startled deer may race across the road. Deer also seldom travel alone. If you see one, there are typically more nearby.

# WHITE-TAILED DEER

Unlike the nondescript tail of the mule deer, the bounding white-tailed deer *(Odocoileus virginianus)* holds its tail up like a white flag, signaling other deer that it may be time to flee. The unmistakable beacon also helps fawns keep track of their mothers while on the run.

White-tailed deer, with a slight build, usually stand a bit shorter than mule deer and prefer woodland habitat with good cover for hiding. Their vision and hearing is superb, making it difficult for predators to surprise them. Their coats take on a reddish tint in summer that fades into slate gray during the winter. The coats are adorned by white trim in spots such as their muzzles and inside their ears. The male white-tailed deer's antlers curve forward, with each tine branching off the main beam, and may hold a different shape on each side. They shed antlers and grow new ones each year, a process that may consume lots of energy, but which also defines a buck's breeding success. Like elk and bison bulls, buck deer that may weigh as much as 300 pounds challenge each other for the attention of does, which bear either one, two or—rarely—three spotted fawns in the early summer.

Bucks mark their territories by scraping their antlers against trees and typically seek out all does within their domain. Whitetails supplied Indians and early settlers with food and clothing. The deer themselves have varied diets including grass, twigs, leaves and other vegetation.

## Where To Find White-tailed Deer

Look in open parks, especially at the forest's edge and near water. When they feel threatened, deer will often stand stone still, making it difficult to pick them out from the background. White-tailed deer reside in all three parks, especially along river bottoms in Theodore Roosevelt National Park.

## BLACK-TAILED PRAIRIE DOG

If any one species could be considered the socialite of the prairie, it's probably the diminutive black-tailed prairie dog *(Cynomys ludovicianus)*. The busy, burrowing rodents colonize grasslands just as we establish the neighborhoods in which we live. Prairie dog towns are the ultimate in community planning. Towns are divided into different neighborhoods—what biologists call "wards"—each of which is home to several families. While each family is led by a dominant male defensive about his territory, animals within the families are endlessly social. You might notice them grooming each other, playing, chewing or carrying grasses, kissing (actually a kind of greeting display among family members), digging new holes or standing together atop their distinctive mounds, surveying their domains.

Prairie dog towns are hard to miss. They contain hundreds or thousands of animals and often stretch over 100 acres or more, which will be apparent because vegetation throughout the town is as closely cropped as a putting green. There are two reasons for this. First and most obvious, prairie dogs need to eat. But they will also mow down larger plants like sagebrush so they have a clear view of their surroundings and any predators that might be slinking about. Trying to recover its lost ground, the vegetation then grows more vigorously, which may attract bison, deer and other animals in pursuit of extra food.

This rarely bothers the prairie dogs. While they seem to enjoy romping on the surface, they spend much of their life underground. A shallow listening station usually sits just beneath the mound that contains the main entrance to their burrow. Prairie dogs may wait there to make sure the surface is safe before heading up. Below that lies a main chamber where the family rests and where litters of four to five young are born in the spring. Black-tailed prairie dogs, one of five species of prairie dogs and so-called because of their tail's black tip, do not hibernate, but they do spend much of the winter in their burrow, living off stored food. Underground tunnels may connect several different burrows so inhabitants have ready-made escape routes if a predator should pounce.

When prairie dogs on the surface sense danger, they sound a loud chirp, or bark, which tells you how the animals got their name. If you listen to their calls, you may notice different varieties. Other cries may be territorial warnings or "all clear" signals.

A reminder: However tempting, avoid feeding prairie dogs you come across. Human food disrupts their natural diet and may even kill them. It will also turn them from the wild, inquisitive animals you want to see in national parks into a kind of overfed, domestic pet. By resisting the urge, you will also protect yourself; prairie dogs will scratch and bite. They may carry the plague and other diseases dangerous to humans.

## Where To Find Black-tailed Prairie Dogs

It might be easier to describe where *not* to find prairie dogs, since the lively rodents are so abundant. The Roberts Prairie Dog Town along the Sage Creek Rim Road in Badlands National Park is one of the most impressive in size, but there are also large colonies near the visitor center turnoff in Wind Cave National Park (Prairie Dog Canyon lies nearby) and at several points along the loop road in the South Unit of Theodore Roosevelt National Park (here you may notice prairie dogs coated with black dust from burrowing through coal seams).

## COYOTE

It may be the one sound that most typifies the Wild West—the yips and yelps and then the fading howl of the coyote *(Canis latrans)*. The crafty predators, relatives of the domestic dog, exist almost everywhere in the West despite decades of intensive government and private programs aimed at trimming their numbers to halt their occasional attacks on livestock.

Although it might seem so, coyotes do not howl at the moon; their howls are actually just one element in an elaborate canine language that contains many different calls with many different intents, from summoning relatives and broadcasting one's presence to other, unrelated coyotes, to identifying danger and even showing affection.

Like most domestic dogs, coyotes are very social, usually roaming in packs that might range from just a pair of adults to several. Coyotes make their homes in dens often dug into the sides of canyons or along riverbanks, but they may travel many miles away when searching for food. They have the stature of medium-sized dogs with gray coats that might be tinted with brown or red. A bushy tail with a black tip hangs down toward the ground when they run; as opposed to wolves, which hold their tails straight out behind them. There are no wolves, however, in these three national parks.

Coyotes often mate for life. They breed in late winter; the female gives birth to pups in her den in April or May. Biologists believe the number of pups may be determined by the abundance of food and density of the local coyote population, although it is not clear just how the system works. When there are few other coyotes to compete with and food is plentiful, females may bear a dozen or more young; in extraordinary cases, the total may be as high as twenty. When the coyote population is thick and prey populations are limited, the female may produce only a few pups, or maybe none at all.

As the West was settled and developed, wolves and coyotes both faced trapping and poisoning campaigns financed largely by the federal government in defense of stockmen. Wolves vanished, but coyotes lived on and, in fact, flourished, expanding their range to include many eastern states. In the absence of wolves, coyotes also moved up the biological pyramid to become the dominant predator in many parts of the West. Coyote control campaigns continue to this day, although not in national parks.

The coyote is an opportunist in nearly everything it does. Families may set up house wherever it's convenient, be it the edge of a city or a remote mountainside. Coyotes eat whatever is handy, from grasshoppers, berries, rodents and rabbits to deer, antelope and even elk. While coyotes may not specifically try to kill young, old or sickly deer, it often works out that way, because those are the animals that are easiest to bring down. In that way, coyotes help balance populations of other species.

## Where To Find Coyotes

Think like a coyote and look in places a coyote would be apt to go. They may often be seen stalking through prairie dog towns in search of an easy meal or moving along dry washes where they might scare up a rabbit or two. Look carefully, though, for they blend into the badlands and grassland terrain throughout all three parks. Concentrate on prairie expanses, particularly at dawn.

## BLACK-FOOTED FERRET

Perhaps the black-footed ferret *(Mustela nigripes)* best mirrors the changes wrought on the western landscape during the last century. Hunters of nothing but prairie dogs, ferrets may have numbered in the millions at a time when prairie dog towns stretched for miles. Then prairie dogs thinned in advance of livestock and human development, to the point where they now occupy less than 5 percent of their original habitat. Following the curve of prairie dog populations was the black-footed ferret, now the rarest North American animal and one of the rarest species in the world.

Badlands National Park is one of the very few places where biologists are pursuing a strategy they hope will bring the ferret back from the brink of extinction. The charismatic creatures have black socks and masks that make them look like little bandits. The Sioux Indian name for the ferret is *"pispiza etopta sapa"*—"the black-faced one." Since ferrets are entirely dependent on the prairie dog, their future is inextricably linked with that of their prey. As they hunt prairie dogs, ferrets take over the dog burrows as their own to raise litters of about six young born in the spring. It's difficult to sight a ferret, since the animals are sly, scarce and active mostly at night. Ounce for ounce, though, black-footed ferrets are extremely efficient predators. About the size of a human's forearm, they seize prairie dogs with lightning attacks to the neck and then drag away their prize, which often weigh more than they do.

Unfortunately, ferrets live on a tightrope. Their prey goes through wild population swings due to disease. They also live a hazardous life, vulnerable to diseases and predators of their own. Those may have led to the decline of a South Dakota ferret population, east of Badlands National Park, that at the time held the last-known black-footed ferrets on Earth. To safeguard a few animals, in 1971 biologists caught six ferrets and promptly inoculated them for disease, but the vaccine unexpectedly killed four of the six. As the numbers of wild ferrets plummeted, teams trapped three more animals in a desperate attempt to save the species, but the captive animals produced only a few young, which died within days of birth. The last captive died in 1979. With it went many people's last hope of ever seeing the masked one again.

As it often does, though, nature sprung a surprise two years later

when a ranch dog in western Wyoming came home with a black-footed ferret in its mouth. As researchers descended on the newfound colony, protected under the Endangered Species Act, ferret numbers again fell into a downward spiral. Captured animals died, leaving only a very few in the wild. Determined to salvage the species, biologists caught every last known wild ferret and then, working with 18 captive animals, coaxed ferret numbers back into the hundreds. Many of the offspring have been released in Badlands National Park and a few other hand-picked spots. The reintroduced animals have produced kits; the future of the species rests on the shoulders of these young animals.

## Where To Find Black-footed Ferrets

No ferret release sites are easily accessible; most are located in the Sage Creek Wilderness. During certain parts of the year, ferret release sites are closed to all but park biologists. You must be prepared to hike at least eight miles round-trip during evening hours to get to these spots. Check at the Ben Reifel Visitor Center for current information. A few ferrets have been sighted in prairie dog towns within view of park roads. If you see one, let rangers know, for they are tracking the animals carefully. Ranger programs and visitor center displays can tell you more about the species' current status.

## BEAVER

If monuments like Hoover Dam impress you, consider the beaver. Besides people, beavers *(Castor canadensis)* probably do more to engineer their surroundings to their liking more than any other species on Earth. They are nature's engineer, building miniature Hoover Dams in a day or two, turning rolling sections of rivers and streams into placid ponds where they may then hold sway. These same ponds create new wetlands, which grow more succulent vegetation, which attracts songbirds and deer, elk and anything else that is hungry.

Beavers can be credited with fueling the early exploration of the West, much of which was conducted by trappers collecting valuable beaver pelts. Beaver populations suffered in the process, but after gaining government protection in the early 1900s, the species recovered and resumed its engineering feats. Seeing and hearing flowing water seems to compel beavers to set up a construction zone. They begin by chopping down trees along the water's edge with their chisel-like front teeth; after pruning the logs, they roll them into the river and float them downstream. A single beaver may cut down 200 to 300 trees each year. Many become the superstructure for dams, which beavers build out of whatever is available—trees, branches, rocks, even bottles and aluminum cans. In the center of the resulting reservoirs are mound-type lodges of sticks and mud where beavers make their home, although families living along swift-flowing rivers will dig dens in the riverbanks. Lodges and dens usually have at least two underwater entrances, so beavers can get in and out even when the ponds and rivers are frozen over. They cache submerged piles of tree and shrub branches nearby and feast on them through the winter, when other food is unavailable.

If you spot a beaver, you will see how well-adapted the species is to its watery haunts. Oil rubbed into their thick fur makes their coats as water repellent as a newly waxed car. Even when they are swimming, their skin stays dry. Webbed hind feet make beavers Olympic-class swimmers and their flat, fur-free tail serves as a rudder and propeller when necessary. Slapping the water's surface, the tail can also sound a danger alarm. A beaver's nostrils and ears both seal themselves underwater. The creatures are rather awkward on land and rarely stray far from their aquatic refuge.

Beavers mate for life, living in family groups that build and maintain their own network of dams and canals, which they mark with scent to identify it as their territory. Adult beavers may weigh more than 50 pounds. Mating once each winter, beavers give birth in late spring to an average two to four young that already have coats of fur and may start swimming near the lodge within their first hour out of the womb. Young beavers usually stay with their family for two years before striking out on their own.

## Where To Find Beavers

To view beavers, the watchword is water. Beaver habitat is limited in the arid West, but the adept divers may be seen along reliable watercourses such as the Little Missouri River in both units of Theodore Roosevelt National Park and Squaw Creek in the North Unit. Despite its name, beavers have not lived in Beaver Creek in Wind Cave National Park for decades. Beavers are seen rarely along a few scattered creeks in the Sage Creek region of Badlands National Park.

## BIGHORN SHEEP

Renowned naturalist John James Audubon was surveying the West in 1843 when he sighted a band of twenty-five bighorn sheep *(Ovis canadensis)* clambering across the buff-colored badlands of modern-day South Dakota. The animals Audubon saw were actually a bighorn subspecies native only to the clay badlands and low river breaks of North and South Dakota. Their scientific name, *Ovis canadensis audobonii*, paid tribute to Audubon.

A band of 30 or so bighorn sheep frequented the Badlands National Park region from 1908 to 1909, but were eliminated as competition after a domestic sheep operation was established nearby. Others were seen clattering amid the high reaches of the Black Hills, but they too vanished, probably due to overhunting and disease passed on by domestic livestock. By about 1921, the Audubon bighorn had disappeared.

But Rocky Mountain bighorn sheep, a close relative of the local subspecies (some biologists believe the two are so genetically similar they are essentially the same species), were released to repopulate Badlands National Park in 1964. California bighorns were freed in Theodore Roosevelt National Park. Each transplant had mixed success. Bighorns survive in both parks (providing prey for coyotes and mountain lions), but not in numbers anywhere near their original populations.

Bighorn sheep are a study in agility. They sure-footedly scale cliffsides that look like they would give high-wire acrobats vertigo. Hooves that are hard around the edge but spongy in the center work like tennis shoes to give bighorns good traction on even the most slippery-sheer rock. But it is the curling, corkscrew horns that stand out most. Ewes carry relatively short and thin horns, but mature rams may carry crowns that form full curls and sometimes even exceed full curls—forcing the rams to shave off the ends by rubbing them against rocks, lest they obscure their owners' vision. During the fall rut, or breeding season, rams clash for access to ewes with head-butting jousts that might run 20 hours or more. Ewes bear single lambs in the spring and early summer. Lambs and other young sheep travel in female-led herds that munch on grasses and sedges through the summer; in winter, rams join up, often expanding the herd to 100 or more, and bighorn appetites turn to woody plants.

## Where To Find Bighorn Sheep

Watch brush-covered hillsides steep enough to give bighorns refuge from predators and green enough to supply them with food. Bighorns roam the rugged Pinnacles section in the west end of Badlands National Park and the rough, water-carved hillsides of the North Unit of Theodore Roosevelt National Park. Biologists plan to reintroduce bighorns to other sections of Badlands National Park.

# PRONGHORN

When most species of large, vegetarian wildlife—elk and deer, for instance—detect danger, they retreat to the forest, seeking shelter within the trees. Not the pronghorn *(Antilocapra americana)*. When the pronghorn needs to escape, it heads straight out into the open and uses its uncanny speed to leave most any pursuer in the dust.

Pronghorn, or pronghorn antelope as they are often called, rank as the fastest animal in the Western Hemisphere and are truly the speedsters of the prairie. They can cruise along at 30 miles per hour for 15 miles or more, top 45 mph when necessary and can even hit 70 mph in short bursts. Each one of their bounds may stretch 20 feet. You may notice that pronghorn run with their mouths open, gulping oxygen to fuel their muscles.

Clearly pronghorn get their name from their signature horns. Shaped like jagged sickles, the horns of bucks extend up to two feet, curving toward each other, and are replaced each year. Does also have horns, which usually are no more than a few inches long. Pronghorn colors are also distinctive: reddish-tan along the back and outer legs, with their undersides white and zebra-like striations across their necks. Bucks weighing an average of 125 pounds assemble harems of does during the fall breeding season; does give birth to one fawn in May or June following their first breeding season and usually twins or triplets in succeeding years. Air-filled hairs fringe their coats, affording extra insulation against icy winters. Since antelope spend so much time in the open, eating plenty of sagebrush, their young are often vulnerable to predators such as coyotes and even golden eagles. Their speed is not much help if it will leave helpless fawns behind. Another fatal flaw is the pronghorn's intense curiosity; early hunters learned they could simply wave a white bandanna to attract the animals within shooting range.

Herds of bison that once roamed the plains churned up the earth, prompting growth of more weedy, broad-leafed plants preferred by pronghorn, so the two species sometimes traveled together. Pronghorn suffered from the same pressures that led to the downfall of other prairie wildlife, but they are one of the few animals that has recovered. There may be 1 million or more roaming the West today, with populations in some spots, especially national parks, that approach their original numbers.

## Where To Find Pronghorns

Look in open grassland sections, where pronghorn coats blend with the bronze grasses in the morning and afternoon. They usually can be seen along the road and trails in the southern section of Wind Cave National Park, in fields between Big Foot and Dillon passes in Badlands National Park and on clay ridges in both units of Theodore Roosevelt National Park.

# MOUNTAIN LION

There probably isn't a more finely tuned hunting machine than the mountain lion *(Felis concolor)*, also known as cougar, puma or panther. Its lean, muscle-bound, six-foot body is suited for swift but short sprints that may include 45-foot bounds and 20-foot vertical leaps up a sheer rock face. Sharp claws are normally retracted for silent stalking, but quickly extended for rapid attack. Sensitive whiskers detect obstacles, averting a noisy collision that would alert prey. A short, compact jaw maximizes the crushing power of the cat's 30 teeth, while a rough tongue allows the lion to clean every last bit of meat from the bones of its prey.

By virtue of its profession, the "cat of one color" as its scientific name says, is usually invisible, but its role in the grassland ecosystem is very much in evidence. Hunting pressure from these cats and other large predators keeps the antelope and deer you see alert and, through the millennia, has also forced them to develop such admirable evasive skills as the pronghorn's lightning-quick speed. To counteract such talents, the mountain lion depends on surprise in its attacks on deer, porcupines, coyotes, beavers and others, which is why it is unusual for a lion to show itself. National Park Service researchers have found 300-pound elk killed and dragged away by a single, 90-pound female mountain lion. The cats may shroud such kills under branches and leaves so they can return day after day to feed.

But despite their secrecy, lions are highly territorial, so they may scratch or gouge trees in their terrain and leave small mounds of pine needles and debris marked with urine or feces as signposts that tell other lions, "No vacancy." For many years, though, it was humans who tried to show mountain lions the door, hunting and trapping them to limit their dining on livestock. Even Theodore Roosevelt disliked what he called the "big horse-killing cat, destroyer of the deer and lord of stealthy murder with a heart craven and cruel." While lion numbers are diminished, they never declined to the point of extinction, as did many wolf and grizzly bear populations. The species is generally strong in the American West, especially in national parks.

The four-toed tracks of mountain lions resemble those of house cats, a distant relative. The cats themselves are tawny brown with a long tail and often weigh 100 to 200 pounds. They socialize only to mate and litters of up to six spotted cubs are born most often in mid-summer in the shelter of caves, crevices or other dens. Cubs usually stay with their mother for a year or more, learning the ways of the wild before setting off on their own. It is these young, unschooled cats that have been implicated in scattered attacks on people, whom they probably mistook for prey. For this reason, if you see a mountain lion and feel threatened, do not run. If you do, you will look like prey. Instead, show your dominance by yelling in an authoritative voice, waving your arms and throwing rocks and sticks.

## Where To Find Mountain Lions

Since mountain lions typically avoid people, you can consider yourself lucky if you see one. If you do, it's probably unintentional on the lion's part. Do not approach. Lions occur throughout each national park; you may find their tracks after brief rainstorms.

## BOBCAT

Look closely at the face of the bobcat *(Felis rufus)* and within it you may see the visage of your own house cat. Although bobcats tend to be slightly larger than domesticated cats and wear longer and more distinctly spotted fur, the two are closely related. Bobcats are the most abundant wild cat in North America, ranging from the East to West Coasts, from Canada south into Mexico.

Like mountain lions, bobcats are especially adept hunters. Their tracks may look like they were left by some sort of strange two-legged, sharply clawed cat, because no rear paw-prints show up. This is because the bobcat often places its rear feet precisely within the tracks left by its front feet. Biologists suspect that this mechanism may give the bobcat a competitive advantage when hunting: once the animal quietly places its front feet, its rear feet go right in the same silent spots. As hunters, bobcats mainly operate at night and are well camouflaged. Their gray,

50

mottled coats, with a faint hint of leopard-like spots, make them nearly invisible while they wait atop a boulder or in the lower branches of a tree for potential prey on which to pounce.

Cottontail and jack rabbits, mice, squirrels, other rodents and birds are the bobcat's typical prey. Bobcats stake out hunting territories, one per cat, which they mark by urinating or clawing telltale scratches into a tree. They tend to avoid open areas and broad plains with little hunting cover. Territories exclude other bobcats of the same sex, but territories of male and female bobcats may overlap. Still, bobcats typically live alone except during the late winter mating season and when mothers are caring for their two- to three-kitten litters. Male cats are polygamous, so one male may mate with several females, although the equation does not work the other way around. Kittens, born in April and May, learn to hunt when they are about six months old, and by the age of 12 months usually leave their mothers to find their own territories.

The bobcat gets its name from its stubby, "bobbed" tail that contrasts with the longer, undulating tail of a house cat.

## Where To Find Bobcats

Usually hunting in the dusk-to-dawn hours, bobcats are rarely seen. They prefer the rough terrain at Cliff Shelf, Sage Creek and Norbeck Ridge in Badlands National Park. They may also be sighted in the South Unit of Theodore Roosevelt National Park in the vicinity of the Ridgeline Nature Trail. Like prairie dogs, Theodore Roosevelt bobcats may sometimes appear dark when they den within coal seams.

## RED FOX

Silent stalkers, foxes rarely show themselves even where they are numerous. Although sly, the red fox *(Vulpes vulpes)* is common enough to be seen in the national parks. They are shy animals. They dig their dens and give birth underground or in the alcoves of hollow trees or rock piles and are active mostly at night, when their large eyes help them navigate through the dark.

Foxes are primarily predators and will make meals out of almost anything they can catch—rodents (especially prairie dogs), rabbits, birds, lizards and insects, even scorpions—although they may turn to vegetation when hungry. Small in stature, they are distinguished by thick, lustrous fur that was once in high demand for fur coats. Compared to larger predators such as wolves, coyotes and bears, foxes have earned less human enmity, probably because they do not pose as great a threat to domestic livestock, aside from the occasional chicken coop. They run quickly—25 miles per hour or more—bounding in graceful arcs that make it look as if they are bouncing on a pillow of air.

Different species of foxes fit the same mold. They are about the size of a German Shepherd puppy, although their bushy tails are thick and nearly as long as their bodies and may brush their tracks away as they travel. During snowstorms, foxes might simply wrap themselves in their luxuriously thick tail to keep warm. Fox ears are large and prominent, all the better to hear you with. It's mainly foxes' color that distinguishes their kind. Swift foxes are smaller and usually appear brown-gray with a black-tipped tail. Red foxes are, as you might guess, red, although they may actually sport a variety of color schemes running from black to silver to red and everywhere in between. In all cases, though, red fox tails have white tips.

Red foxes tend toward mixed wooded regions with more hiding cover. Male and female foxes pair up in the fall and mate during winter. Come spring, the females give birth to litters averaging about five pups in shallow dens. Males usually do not den with their mates and young, but they may help raise pups once the pups leave the den.

## Where To Find Red Foxes

Since foxes are mostly nocturnal, they can be difficult to spot, but they roam all three parks. Look amid the high grass of the prairie and prairie dog towns, where they might be stalking dinner. Watch also while driving at night, since you will probably see the green reflections of a fox's eyes before anything else.

# REPTILES & AMPHIBIANS

## PRAIRIE RATTLESNAKE

It's an unmistakable sound: a furious buzzing like a child's rattle on fast-forward, but which puts anyone's heart on edge. Hearing a rattlesnake's rattle is not necessarily a sign you are in danger, but it is a warning, and should be taken as such. Rattlesnakes probably do not want to be in your way any more than you want to be in their way, so they shake the rattle at the tip of their tail not to provoke a confrontation, but to avoid one. Be mindful of that and you should be safe.

The prairie rattlesnake *(Crotalus viridis viridis)* is a subspecies of the far-ranging western rattlesnake, which can be found in every western state and averages three to four feet long. The western rattlesnake is a member of the pit viper family and yes, it is poisonous. But its venom is designed to work on its prey, which does not include people, so its bite usually is not fatal to humans. Sometimes when rattlesnakes bite people, no venom is injected.

But the same calming words cannot apply to the rattlesnake's prey, which includes rats, mice and other rodents, as well as birds. Rattlers usually lie in wait beneath bushes or rocks and strike when an unassuming victim passes by, using their venom to gain the upper hand. The snakes swallow their prey whole and may go days until their next meal.

Because reptiles are cold-blooded and cannot regulate their body heat as mammals can, their internal temperature is controlled by their surroundings, so they must seek out

places that are comfortable. In the summer, this means shade, perhaps among rocks or low brush; the hot sun would kill an exposed rattler in less than a half-hour. So rattlesnakes do much of their hunting at night or in the morning and evening, when the air cools. Lower temperatures also make them more effective hunters, since they can then rely on their "pits," that look like their nostrils but which are actually super-sensitive temperature sensors that can detect temperature differences as small as one-tenth of a degree. Differences, for instance, that might tip them off to a warm-blooded mouse scurrying by.

The skin of rattlers is tan-gray, with a line of blotches that may look like diamonds or squares running down the back, edged by gray or black. At the end of the rattler's tail is its famous noisemaker, which is basically a string of what look like kernels of corn that each hold a bead-like rattle inside. When a rattlesnake feels threatened, it coils up, raises its head and vibrates its tail to sound the alarm. Each time a rattler sheds its skin, made of material similar to your fingernails, a new rattle appears. Since snakes do not shed exactly once a year, the number of rattles is not a precise count of a snake's age, but it can serve as a relative estimate. While most snakes lay eggs, rattlesnakes give birth to live youngsters.

### Where To Find Prairie Rattlesnakes

You may *not* want to find rattlesnakes, but stay on the lookout for them amid mixed grass and on rocky and talus slopes in all three parks. Watch the ground and do not put your hands or feet anywhere you cannot see them. Wear long pants and boots. Prairie dog and other rodent burrows may harbor snakes. In winter, many rattlesnakes hibernate together in such holes.

# BULLSNAKE

At first glance, the bullsnake *(Pituophis melanoleucus sayi)*, also called the gopher snake, may look like a rattler—it has the same dark diamond-like shapes down its back. But there are several important differences. The bullsnake is not venomous, is more numerous, has no rattles on its tail, has a head that is not as flat as the rattler's, and is often much longer than its poisonous relative—four to six feet on

average and sometimes as long as eight feet.

Bullsnakes are powerfully built, often as wide as a person's fist, and make their living off rodents; they often serve to control popula- tions of gophers, rats and mice. They live in very diverse surroundings, from Canada south to Mexico, west to California and east to the Great Lakes, doing just as well in rocky deserts as in sheltered woodlands. Although they are not poisonous, bullsnakes can be aggressive. When threatened, they often produce a frighteningly loud hiss, sometimes flattening their heads and vibrating their tail, as if they are trying to call upon the scare-power of their more ominous, rattling cousins.

Bullsnakes are most active during the day, but in hot weather may postpone their slitherings until sundown. After mating in the spring, they bear up to two dozen creamy white eggs in summer in sheltered spots such as sandy burrows or underneath rocks or logs. The eggs hatch in two to three months.

## Where To Find Bullsnakes

These scale-sided creatures can be found almost anywhere and are most easily seen while walking national park trails. Watch low vegetation for an inkling of movement that might reveal a snake. Bullsnakes are common near Badlands National Park's Cedar Pass and Sage Creek campgrounds, where they prey upon rodents attracted by human litter.

## GREAT PLAINS TOAD

While the arid grasslands of the Dakotas may not seem like toad-friendly places, shallow sloughs and streambeds often hold all the amphibian necessities: moisture, insects to eat, and loose soil that offers cool refuge on hot summer days. Toads do not actually require running water—in fact they may prefer drier spots where burrowing into the earth is easier.

The Great Plains toad (*Bufo cognatus*) has trill-like calls that usually come about once each second. It has bony ridges on its snout and skin and is covered with gray-brown tubercles, which are the wart-like bumps for which toads are known and are incorrectly thought by some to give handlers warts. They do not. But toads can secrete bad-tasting and sometimes toxic substances designed to keep predators from eating them. There is another real reason to treat toads respect-fully: Frogs, toads and other amphibians have been the victims of mysterious declines around the world. Researchers are not sure why, but speculate on a wide variety of possible causes, from global climate change to loss of habitat. Toads and their relatives need our respect and protection if they are to survive.

When the Great Plains toad feels threatened, it closes its eyes, puffs up its body and lowers its head, ending up looking like a green-gray rock. Like most amphibians, the Great Plains toad is nocturnal and lays its eggs in water, where the eggs turn into swimming tad-poles and, later, hopping toad offspring.

## Where To Find Great Plains Toads

While toads do not spend their entire lives in water, they usually reside in places where some moisture is available, such as near fire hydrants, restrooms and water fountains. They may spend hot days burrowed into the soil—try not to bother them, for they need their energy during their nighttime searches for insect meals. They are typi-cally present in all three parks, mainly in moist stream bottoms.

# BIRDS

## TURKEY VULTURE

Black shapes turning lazy circles in the sky—the image is familiar to anyone who has watched old western movies. Some call the shallow V-shapes buzzards, but they are properly known as turkey vultures *(Cathartes aura)*. They survive where other animals cannot, or will not, by taking eager advantage of the misfortune of other wildlife. While vultures are one of the continent's largest birds of prey, they zero in on weak, dying or dead animals.

Their leathery red heads, devoid of feathers, let them eat unhindered from the carcasses of others. It may seem disgusting, but vultures fill a role in the harsh badlands or wide grasslands by recycling the flesh of dead animals back into the living. They are so used to eating dead meat, their claws are no good for grasping prey. Their sense of smell is keener than that of most other birds, and they use it to seek out carrion.

You are most likely to see vultures weaving above, which does not mean they see you as a promising meal. They may simply be on the lookout, and if they see you walking, they will fly on by. You can tell turkey vultures from other large birds because their necks appear very short and their separate wingtip feathers form a ragged fan—like your hand when you spread out your fingers. Their black-brown wings may stretch six feet across, a span that lets them glide long distances without much effort, a useful skill on hot summer days that send other creatures into hiding.

Vultures are common from early spring to late fall, but they leave the plains for the winter. They nest and roost in groups on rocky cliffs or steep slopes or even tall trees without many leaves to obscure their view. Once they take off, vultures do not seem to be in any hurry— and they are not. They will wait as long as it takes.

### Where To Find Turkey Vultures

Look up on most summer days and you will eventually see a vulture, or even a flock, cruising over. In the morning, watch ridgetops and trees for vultures warming their wings in the first sun, and in the evening, watch for them soaring toward the spires of the badlands where they roost. The large formation directly across from the Ben Reifel Visitor Center in Badlands National Park is called Vulture Peak, because many vultures nest there.

## RED-TAILED HAWK

The most common hawk on the Great Plains is probably the red-tailed hawk *(Buteo jamaicensis)*, a relative of the vulture. The hawk wears a careful, intent look on its face, as if it is always scrutinizing the landscape for a tempting rodent or even a dead or dying animal that might serve as a meal. Red-tails adapt easily to human trappings: you may see them stone still atop a telephone pole, sign or fence post, and then, in a second, they can be in the air, diving after a lizard, mouse or squirrel racing across the ground.

With a wingspan of four to five feet, red-tails are large hawks that are most often dark brown above and lighter brown or cream-colored below. The broad, brownish-red tail has a narrow dark band and a buffy tip. A variation of red-tail common to the Great Plains is much lighter in color, with a very light brown or tan tail, probably to better blend into the golden grass of the prairie. Younger birds are also light in color, with a whitish breast lined by narrow brown bands.

Red-tailed hawks live in almost any environment, from alpine meadows to dusty deserts, although they may migrate south from northern climes in the winter. Courtship flights are dramatic, with the mating pair sometimes interlocking their talons and somersaulting down through the sky before separating, recovering and then flying off.

They build their nests in seclusion where they can—tall trees, high brush, cacti or cliffs. The female stays with her typical two to three eggs while the male looks for food; eggs usually hatch in about a month. Their cry is at first hoarse, turning into a drawn-out scream that is often used in the movies to imitate the much rarer cry of an eagle.

## Where To Find Red-tailed Hawks

Watch vantage points where a hawk might be resting, watching for potential prey. Promising spots in all three parks include stream-bottoms or thick grasses where food is likely to be plentiful. They are common along fence rows bordering Badlands National Park.

63

### GOLDEN EAGLE

With an average wingspan of six to seven feet, the golden eagle *(Aquila chrysaetos)* is one of the few birds to approach the turkey vulture in size; you can tell the difference between the two species as they soar far overhead because the feathers at the tip of the vulture's wings are spread apart like spikes, while those of the eagle's wing remain together in a solid point.

The golden eagle is largely dark brown, but its head and neck usually run toward bronze or gold. Its yellow talons are impressive—they often are as broad as a human palm. That and its size make the golden eagle a preeminent predator. It typically searches out rabbits and other large rodents with eyes that approximate powerful binoculars, but may also zoom down at speeds approaching 100 miles per hour and grab unwary deer or antelope fawns, especially those struggling in a spring snowstorm or other adverse conditions. Goldens have been known to carry away prey weighing nearly 10 pounds, almost as heavy as the adult eagles themselves. Ranchers worry about goldens going after newborn lambs, and goldens were often subject to hunting campaigns in decades past, although their overall toll on livestock may not be great compared to other predators such as coyotes and foxes.

Golden eagles will use the same nests on cliff ledges or high trees year after year, re-lining them with twigs and green vegetation. Both male and female eagles take their turns incubating the average two white eggs that usually hatch in about 45 days during the spring months. Young goldens first fly at about 12 weeks of age—they can be distinguished from adults by a white patch on each wing and a whitish tail as well. Golden eagles residing on the plains usually do not migrate, although they may range farther in search of food. It is unusual to hear golden eagles sound their cry, a high screech.

## Where To Find Golden Eagles

Study the nooks and crannies of cliffs and tall trees for bulky nests. Golden eagles usually sweep the sky alone. They are not easily seen, but in Badlands National Park are most visible near Cliff Shelf and Sage Creek. A mounted golden eagle hangs in the visitor center in the North Unit of Theodore Roosevelt National Park.

## BALD EAGLE

Nobody can mistake the bald eagle *(Haliaeetus leucocephalus)*, America's national bird since 1782. The bird's most striking feature is its stark white head atop a body of dark brown. Aside from the distinguished head, the bald eagle basically resembles its relative, the golden eagle. Because bald eagles do not attain their white crown until they are at least three years old, juveniles may look at first like golden eagles, although the young balds are lighter in color and more grayish than the very dark brown goldens.

Perhaps the main difference between the two species is that bald eagles generally live around water, preferring fish and carrion to other prey. This means the Great Plains are generally a dry sea that bald eagles cross on their way north in warmer months and south in colder months. But in spring and fall, you may spot a distinctive bald eagle, especially perched in cottonwood trees along rivers like the Little Missouri in Theodore Roosevelt National Park. Since the bald is not much of a predator compared to its golden cousin, Benjamin Franklin complained that the bald eagle was not a fitting choice as the national bird. Being "a bird of bad moral character," Franklin said, "he does not get his living honestly." But Franklin's view obviously did not carry much weight with those who have seen the bald eagle perched regally in a tree or streaking over the water, snatching a fish with its talons.

Bald eagles mate for life and build their nests in high trees or cliffs, improving them with new twigs and sticks each year. Eagle nests that have been in use for 15 years might weigh more than a ton. Usually only two chicks are born in the spring of each year, leaving bald eagles only a very slim opportunity to maintain their populations when toxic pesticides began contaminating the fish they ate, and, unavoidably, the eagles themselves. The bald eagle received government protection in 1940, and by 1978 was considered an endangered species in most states. In more recent decades, the species has made a comeback and appears healthy once again.

Fish make up at least half of the bald eagle's diet; where possible, the eagle appears to prefer stealing the catch of ospreys or other fishing birds rather than doing the work itself.

## Where To Find Bald Eagles

Because of the bald eagle's preference for fish, you have the best chance of spotting them along rivers or near streams and ponds. Bald eagles are most numerous when traversing the plains in the spring and fall—look for their telltale shape in leafless trees. Their migrations take them through all three parks.

## MOUNTAIN BLUEBIRD

A striking shade of turquoise, the mountain bluebird *(Sialia currucoides)* is one of the most colorful ornaments to decorate trees on the plains during the very early spring. The female's color is a more muted gray than the male's, but both have whitish abdomens and are about seven inches in length. They are also smooth flyers, with a swallow-like flight plan. Their call is a soft, short warble, while their cry of alarm is a sharper cluck.

Mountain bluebirds nest during March and April in higher meadows with lots of vegetation for cover and drop to the prairies in fall and winter. In the Black Hills and Wind Cave National Park, mountain bluebirds are near the eastern limit of their range. They build their nests in the cavities of trees, rock ledges or in birdhouses. Five or six pale blue eggs is the typical number; chicks hatch after about two weeks and quickly mature. Common bluebird foods include insects, seeds, berries and fruit.

### Where To Find Mountain Bluebirds

Open terrain with scattered brush and trees offers the best chance to spot this blue standout in spring and early summer. Examine the forest's edge, particularly in the northern reaches of Wind Cave National Park.

## BLACK-BILLED MAGPIE

It's not difficult to see a magpie *(Pica pica)*. They are flamboyant show-offs, even down to their coloring. They bear the colors of a domino, jet black on their beaks, backs, wings and super-long tails and snow white on their lower bellies, shoulders and outer flight feathers. They resemble crows and grow to about two feet long. The white feathers turn into a ivory section underneath their wings in flight. Magpies do not hesitate to make their presence known: if their eye-catching appearance does not do it, they will squawk readily in a voice that some describe as a basic *"yak-yak-yak."*

Magpies are not shy and may even try to steal food from picnic tables and other opportune sources. On their own, they mostly eat large insects and other animal matter, although they will consume seeds and fruit if nothing else is available. They seem to enjoy taunting other birds or even larger animals like coyotes by parading by close enough for the others to see the magpies have a meal, but just far enough away that they cannot grab it.

69

Perhaps in keeping with the magpie's personality, its nest looks large and unkempt, although it is actually fairly sturdy. The nest is ball-shaped and built of a big bunch of sticks and branches, some up to six feet long, and is usually located on the ground or in low bushes or trees, especially where thorns deter intruders. The nest is lined on the inside with mud and is so well built that other birds sometimes take it over in subsequent years. A narrow hole on one side leads to a cozy chamber lined with grass and mud. An average of about five or six eggs hatch after about two weeks in the nest and the gray-brown chicks usually leave the nest around June. Magpies generally do not migrate, so they are visible in the national parks throughout the year.

### Where To Find Black-billed Magpies

Magpies are usually anywhere food might be about, even in rugged country. Nests are commonly seen along the Cliff Shelf Nature Trail at the eastern end of Badlands National Park. Do not contribute to the delinquency of magpies: they lose their ability to forage if fed by humans and then, during the harsh winter months when there are fewer visitors, many starve.

# AMERICAN KESTREL

About the size of a common jay, the American Kestrel (Falco sparverius) can attack with a vengeance, and often does, so regularly pouncing on sparrows that it is also known as the sparrow hawk. Its plumage is a rich mix of colors: a rust-colored crown, back and tail, trimmed with black and blue-gray wings. Kestrels are members of the falcon family, but are relatively small in size—no more than a foot long from their heads to the tips of their tails.

The kestrel seems undeterred by human development and even lives in some large cities, feeding on sparrows and other small birds. On the plains, it does the same, often adding rodents and insects to its diet. It's typical to see the kestrel hovering over fields and scrub brush likely to hold food. In winter, kestrels become fewer as many begin migrating south for the very cold months, before returning in early spring.

The call of the kestrel is described as a shrill, rapid-fire "killy, killy, killy" that sets the small bird apart. Kestrels nest in hollow trees or

cacti, often commandeering hideouts used by woodpeckers in previous years. There the females warm an average of four or five eggs without much help from the males. After hatching in or around May, chicks begin to fly in about a month.

## Where To Find American Kestrels

Look for them perched on fence-posts, telephone poles, trees or wires or floating over the prairie, beating their wings quickly to keep up with the breeze. They traverse all of the three parks, but do not stick to any particular landscape.

## HORNED LARK

While most birds build their nests in trees or other elevated spots, the horned lark *(Eremophila alpestris)* is so much a resident of the grasslands that it nests in shallow cups in the ground it lines with grass and feathers. Perhaps due to the vulnerability of the lark's nesting place, its eggs hatch in less than two weeks and within another week or two, the young are airborne.

About seven inches in length and from the same family as the swallow, the horned lark has mostly brown-gray feathers, set off by ripples of white and black on the head. Streaks of black run across the throat, from the beak, past the eye and down to the neck and from the forehead up to the crown, ending there with short, spiky tufts of feathers that are responsible for the bird's name. While flying, the lark's tail looks black with white edges. When traveling on the ground, the horned lark distinguishes itself by walking, not hopping like most of its feathered brethren. Its airborne courtship call sounds like the high tinkling of wind chimes.

The lark feeds mainly on insects in summer and seeds in winter. It is migratory, becoming scarce in winter but returning in large flocks right on the heels of the first signs of spring. Oddly, the lark prefers barren terrain, possibly so approaching predators have no hiding places, for as soon as tall grass takes root, the lark takes off.

## Where To Find Horned Larks

Barren, even desert-like areas without much hiding cover offer the best prospects in all three parks. Watch the broad plains north of the Sage Creek Rim Road in Badlands National Park and along roadsides in Theodore Roosevelt National Park.

## GREAT HORNED OWL

Great horned owls *(Bubo virginianus)* are one of the largest owls in North America, often tall enough to reach a grown person's knee, and their name tells you what to look for to identify them. Two tufts of feathers stick up on either side of the head where it seems their ears might be. The "horns," however, have nothing to do with hearing;

the great horned owl's ears are buried beneath its thick gray-brown and black-striped plumage. It's likely you will hear a great horned owl's deep-throated hooting before you see the animal itself, often a horned shadow at the top of a tall tree at night.

Many cultures have considered owls mystical or supernatural because they appear to accomplish the impossible. They seem to be able to see in the dark, to hear even the faintest rustle of a mouse scampering across the forest floor and then dive silently toward the hapless prey like a rock falling from the sky. In fact, owls are extraordinarily talented because biology and evolution have crafted them to fit their niche in nature almost perfectly.

Although owls are talented birds of prey, they are more closely related to cuckoos and parrots than they are to the hawks and eagles that first come to mind as hunting birds. Owls are nearly all nocturnal, meaning they hunt mostly at night, taking advantage of their keen senses. It is these senses, not supernatural powers, that give owls their extraordinary abilities. Their large eyes collect even the faintest light into a visible image and their conical ear passages funnel every sound into hearing range, so much so that some owls hunt by sound more than they do by sight. And owls themselves make hardly a sound to tip-off potential prey because feathery fringes on the leading edge of their soft and mottled wings dampen the whistling or rustling common to most birds in flight.

The great horned owl is an aggressive predator, eating anything from rabbits to fish and ducks to weasels. Like most owls, its beak is sturdy, with a sharp hook on the end, and its talons are sharp and strong, ideal for tearing flesh from its prey. Indigestible bones and such fall to the ground in pellets beneath the owl's roost. Great horned owls often lay their eggs in nests abandoned by hawks, herons or crows, or build a new nest on cliff ledges or secure spots on the ground. The young stay in the nest for nine or ten weeks before taking their first flight under the watchful, almost scowling eyes of their parents.

## Where To Find Great Horned Owls

Around dusk and dawn, watch trees at the forest's edge and around campgrounds and overlooks, especially where you might wait quietly if you were watching and listening for prey. Great horned owls prowl all the parks—listen for their calls in the Cottonwood Campground in the South Unit of Theodore Roosevelt National Park.

## RED-SHAFTED FLICKER

The Red-shafted flicker *(Colaptes auratus)* is probably the most seen woodpecker on the Great Plains. Flickers are generally about a foot long, with brown backs and heads, black crescents across their breasts and bold black spots on their wings. Males wear bright red stripes on their throats. In flight, their wings appear salmon-pink.

When you hear the drum roll that is a woodpecker drilling its way into a tree in search of ants or grubs, you are hearing the result of one of the more adept adaptations of the bird world. Rather than compete with other birds for common seeds or flying insects, the woodpeckers have devised the tools to bore through solid wood, straight into what is normally a sanctuary for their prey. The chief tool is their beaks, with the seeming strength of steel and tips shaped like chisels. But the rest of their bodies are designed for the same end: short, strong legs that latch onto vertical tree trunks, stiff tails that prop them up while they drill away and long, barbed tongues that stretch deep into a tree like a piece of sticky tape to retrieve bugs.

75

For obvious reasons, woodpeckers are usually found around mature trees and large plants, although they may also probe for food in the soil. Pounding their way into trees is such a big part of their lives that instead of the courtship calls typical of most birds, woodpeckers drum a distinctive rhythm into stumps or boards. Drumming is also a territorial warning. They do have voices, though, which often resemble harsh, cackling laughs that are not all that different from the sounds of their drilling.

Although some species of woodpeckers will move south in winter, they generally do not migrate far. In spring, they drill nesting cavities in trees, posts or even telephone poles and lay about four or five eggs. Both parents care for the youngsters by bringing them food. Nesting holes often serve other birds in later years, making woodpeckers important members of the woodland ecosystem even after they have departed.

### Where To Find Red-shafted Flickers

Scan the trunks of trees, especially in scattered forests, for signs of their workings and listen for their drumming in all three parks. Flickers are less skittish than many other birds, so your chances of seeing one are good.

## WESTERN MEADOWLARK

The western meadowlark *(Sturnella neglecta)* looks so much like the eastern meadowlark that naturalist John James Audubon at first did not notice the difference. When he did, he named the western species "neglecta" because it had long been neglected. Even so, the western meadowlark is difficult to overlook, for it is both common and eye-catching. It has a golden-yellow throat and breast; the breast also bears a V-shaped black stripe. Its wings are largely a combination of brown and gray. The biggest difference between it and its eastern relative is its song, described as a non-stop, flute-like jingling that is nothing like the eastern meadowlark's high-pitched whistling.

You may prefer either one, depending on your ear. Theodore Roosevelt felt the western species gave more melodious performances, and "this I could hardly get used to at first, for it looks exactly like the Eastern meadowlark, which utters nothing but a harsh disagreeable chatter."

Meadowlark courtship rituals do not seem to fit with the bird's peaceful image. Males stake out nesting grounds in early spring and then battle each other by diving and pecking to win access to the arriving females. It's not unusual to see several males chasing a female, who may be flirting with them by fluffing up her feathers or

flashing her wings. Showing their allegiance to the prairie, meadowlarks nest in dugout nooks in the ground, usually in meadows or farm fields, which they cover with an arched roof of interlaced grass and plant stems. Females lay an average of about five spotted eggs in April or May, and the young usually begin flying within less than two weeks. The species feeds most often on insects, grain, seeds and berries. Many meadowlarks head south from the Black Hills and badlands in winter, although enough hang back that it is not that unusual to spot them. Their return in greater numbers is a sure sign of spring.

## Where To Find Western Meadowlarks

The best bet is to inspect open fields and meadows that have a bit of cover in which meadowlarks hide. Look for the flash of yellow from their breast. They flit through all three parks, and may be visible in the scattered woodlands of Wind Cave National Park, and atop fence posts.

## WILD TURKEY

Many may know the turkey as the main course in Thanksgiving feasts, but it is also an important component of woodland ecosystems, picking up and spreading seeds and nuts that give root to new vegetation. Wild turkeys *(Meleagris gallopavo)* tend to have a more streamlined build—slimmer and with longer legs—than domestic turkeys, although they are still large, standing about as tall as, or even taller than, a 10-year-old child.

The wild turkey, also known as the Merriam's turkey, is not native to the Dakotas, but was transplanted to the region as a game bird to provide hunters with more diverse quarry. From about 1948 to 1951,

South Dakota state agencies released imported turkeys throughout the Black Hills. Others were freed in western North Dakota. The birds quickly expanded their numbers and their range so they are now frequently seen in the national parks, clucking and leaning their long necks back-and-forward, back-and-forward as they walk. Wild turkeys were once present across the continent, but human hunting and other pressures drove their numbers down. Now they exist in limited regions and transplant sites like the Dakotas.

While turkeys appear rather peaceable, they can defend themselves well. They can also fly, although it may not appear so, and roost in trees, dropping to the ground during the day to nibble berries, seeds, insects and snails. Males are larger than females, but both have bald, red-blue heads with loose flaps of skin called "wattles" dangling from their necks. During the spring breeding season, male turkeys show off their bronze, fan-like tails to attract a following of females, known as a harem. After mating, the females will incubate their average of about a dozen eggs in depressions on the ground for a month and then raise the young without help from their mates.

## Where To Find Wild Turkeys

Although turkeys are not common in Badlands National Park, they are often seen in Wind Cave and Theodore Roosevelt national parks. Look in scattered-woodland terrain like the northern uplands of Wind Cave and the aptly named Gobbler Ridge to the south.

# GALLERY

## BADGER

Wide and as low-slung as a bulldozer, the badger *(Taxidea taxus)* is built for strength, not speed. Which is appropriate, because badgers prey mainly on other burrowing animals such as prairie dogs and gophers in all three parks. They may often be seen near the Roberts Prairie Dog Town in Badlands National Park. With both hunter and quarry packed face-to-face in an underground tunnel, it is strength and not speed that will win the day.

The badger is well-outfitted for hunting, with a powerful body and short legs topped by sharp claws. Its distinctive colors and white stripe running over its forehead are a danger sign to rodents. Its jaw and sharp teeth can kill a prairie dog in an instant. These carnivores will even take on the rattlesnake, leaving the snake's rattles on the ground outside the entrances to their dens as if they were a trophy. A bit awkward when wandering in search of prey, the badger is much more adept when routing out a burrow to capture and eat the occupants. Sometimes badgers will even dig their way into empty burrows and patiently wait for the meal of the hour to come home. Do not approach badgers; they are ferocious and may bite if threatened.

## PORCUPINE

On first glance at a porcupine *(Erethizon dorsatum)*, you might think it looks like some sort of strange bush with legs. Other animals may see them just the same way, at least until their curiosity gets the best of them and they find themselves turned into living pincushions.

Porcupines are rather clumsy and slow, but who's going to argue with them for holding up traffic? Instead of fast feet or sudden maneuvers, a porcupine carries about 30,000 barbed quills, which are actually long, stiff hairs barely attached to muscles beneath the skin. Porcupines cannot shoot quills, but when they feel threatened, they crouch against the ground, leaving nothing but quills exposed, and slap intruders with their quill-filled tail. Porcupine tracks are obvious in the snow, because they are the ones that look as if they have been swept over with a broom. Females bear one young each year. The young's defenses ensure a high survival rate; baby porcupines emerge with downy-soft quills that harden within hours.

Even trees are not safe around porcupines, but not because of their spiny adornments. Porcupines feed on tree bark and branches at night and, despite their clumsiness on the ground, they are good climbers. If you see bark stripped from conifers, you can bet you are in porcupine country. They have poor eyesight and are frequently found near roadways and pullouts in all three parks. Since they love salt, porcupines seek out wood well-handled by humans, such as doorways, railings and benches.

## RACCOON

If you see what look like tiny human handprints in the snow or mud, you have probably been preceded by a raccoon *(Procyon lotor)*. With a mask of black fur around its eyes and a thick tail with five or so black rings, like the stripes of a prison uniform, the raccoon is often said to look like a little bandit. The description holds true in many cases, for raccoons will watch for any opportunity to steal food from a picnic table or just about anywhere else they can find it. Raccoons dwell in all three parks, especially near the main campgrounds. For this reason, keep your eye on your provisions, especially at night (raccoons are mostly nocturnal). Human food can sicken

81

wildlife, so its loss will do neither you nor the raccoon any good.

It is often said that raccoons wash their food before they eat it. This may be true in some instances, especially when there is water nearby. But if raccoons always held true to the dictum, they would probably spend more time finding a washbasin for their food than eating it. In fact, they are opportunists and will grab any food they can, including, fruit, nuts, bugs, birds' eggs, baby birds and rodents. They are also territorial and will challenge each other with fierce growling in the event they meet up. Raccoons mate in winter and by spring, it's common to see mother raccoons crossing the countryside with around five young following in single file behind her.

## DEER MOUSE

This little creature probably contributes most to the prairie ecosystem in its role as prey for bigger creatures. The deer mouse (*Peromyscus maniculatus*) eats mostly seeds and insects, getting enough moisture from its food that it does not need water, and is itself a staple in the diet of grassland predators. Coyotes and foxes may spend hours pouncing on mice in a field, which looks from a distance to be as much a recreational pursuit for the predators as it is an attempt to find a meal.

Deer mice are one of the widest-ranging and most successful small mammals on the continent, although subspecies in different parts of that range—prairies and woodlands, for instance—carry varying coloration. The woodland variety is larger, with a longer tail and smaller feet, but mice with characteristics of both the woodland and prairie types can be found in places like Wind Cave National Park, where the two ecological zones intersect.

# WHITE-TAILED JACK RABBIT

Imagine a grown human leaping 60 feet across the ground in one jump, around three times the Olympic record for the long jump. That's roughly the human equivalent of the 20-foot distance white-tailed jack rabbits *(Lepus townsendii)* can cover in one leap. Not only that, but they can race across the prairie at speeds of up to 45 miles per hour, fast enough to outrun most predators. Their powerful legs and feet serve another purpose, too: male jackrabbits competing for the attention of females fight by kicking each other violently. They live in all the parks and are often found along the loop road in the South Unit of Theodore Roosevelt National Park.

Jack rabbits got their unusual name because of their tall ears that reminded people of the ears of a male donkey, a jackass. The ears are thoughtfully designed. Not only are they big enough to pull in even the slightest sound of a predator, but they are also criss-crossed by a dense network of blood vessels that radiate excess body heat during hot summer days, keeping the rabbit cool. White-tailed jack rabbits are nocturnal and have grayish-brown fur, which cloaks them by blending in with grasses and sagebrush, especially during the day, when rabbits rest in shallow depressions in the ground. Although called rabbits, jack rabbits are actually hares (and are sometimes called prairie hares), which as a rule give birth to furry young with their eyes already open.

## DESERT COTTONTAIL

Pause at dusk on the rim of the Painted Canyon overlook in the South Unit of Theodore Roosevelt National Park. Once your eyes adjust to the dimming light, scan the ground closely. Chances are good that what seemed like a nondescript gray rock is actually a cottontail rabbit, still as stone. It's the same brave tactic cottontails sometimes use to outwit predators that cannot chase them if they cannot see them. If threatened at close range, though, cottontails dash off, raising their white, cotton-ball tail to alert other rabbits that it's time to take off. When they flee, they often take a zig-zag path designed to confuse predators. Unfortunately, it does not work when the predator is a car speeding at them on a highway.

Desert cottontails *(Sylvilagus audubonii)* are abundant and can easily be seen along the Fossil Exhibit Trail in Badlands National Park. They subsist mostly on grasses, supplemented by sagebrush during the winter. They need not have open water to drink because they manage to extract most of the moisture they need from the foods they eat.

## STRIPED SKUNK

In the vivid language of the wild, the black, bushy tail and body, streaked with twin white stripes coming together atop the head and splitting the face means one thing: Stay away. Animals usually announce themselves with bold coloring only when they have a defensive mechanism potent enough to deter predators. And, if anything, the striped skunk's *(Mephitis mephitis)* defense is mighty potent. When threatened, the skunk aims its tail straight up and blasts a noxious, oily substance from its anal glands toward its perceived threat. Although the substance itself may fly no more than 15 feet or so, the smell might travel a mile or more.

The skunk is not a particularly fast traveler—its walk could better be described as a sort of waddle—but it clearly does not have to be. They can be found in all three parks, particularly along river bottoms. Skunks are typically nocturnal, but they may still venture out during the day from time to time. Skunks reside in underground dens and forage by scraping up bits of earth in search of grubs or other meals. They are also tricky: skunks have been observed rattling beehives to get the bees to leave so they can reach the honey inside. If you are closing in on a skunk, chances are you will smell its thick, musky odor before you see its striking color pattern; if you do, take heed, just as knowledgeable predators should, and back off.

## MINK

Minks *(Mustela vison)* are probably best known as the supplier of lustrous, downy, chocolate-colored pelts for among the most exclusive fur coats. In the wild, though, minks are known for their viciousness. With long and narrow weasel-like bodies (they are actually a type of weasel), minks actually resemble beavers in the respect

that they swim well—aided by webbed toes. Minks effectively hunt water-dwellers including muskrats, fish, turtles and ducks by striking at the neck with their sharp teeth. By virtue of their preferred prey, they are most common along rivers or lakes and marshes. They stake out territories, which are mainly exclusive hunting zones, by marking the boundaries with a scent that smells almost as bad as a skunk's, but is not quite as strong.

85

Male minks, larger than females, are polygamous—that is, they mate with several females each season but end up residing with only one. Minks occur mainly in Theodore Roosevelt National Park, but are difficult to spot even there.

## LONG-TAILED WEASEL

Long-tailed weasels *(Mustela frenata)*, like their cousins the minks, are vicious, especially considering their size. It is an odd twist of nature that weasels occasionally go on murderous rampages, killing animals which they do not eat. It's difficult to know why this happens, since it may be a combination of fact and legend, but somehow the smell of blood appears to motivate weasels; even a bleeding brother or sister may be killed.

When hunting, long-tailed weasels mainly pursue small rodents, but are not put off by larger prey. They are fast, bounding in leaps through the forest, and such good climbers they can overtake a squirrel scurrying up a tree. They will often cache dead mice or other prey in their burrow or some other secure place until they are ready to eat.

Weasels are present in all three parks, but are seldom seen. They mate in midsummer, giving birth to an average of around six or seven young. The long-tailed weasel's back is generally brown and covered with sleek fur, although its underside is white. Its tail makes up about half its total body length. Distinctive white patterns on their face and chin look a little bit like a bridle, which is why the weasel's scientific name includes *"frenata,"* in Latin, "bridle."

## THIRTEEN-LINED GROUND SQUIRREL

The thirteen-lined ground squirrel's *(Spermophilus tridecemlineatus)* markings are so ornate, it looks as if it were decorated by hand. Solid, light-colored stripes run vertically, from head to toe, down its brown back, each one separated from the next by a dotted white line running in the same direction. There may not be exactly 13 lines, but the figure is probably close enough.

Thirteen-lined squirrels are prodigious burrowers and often do not emerge from their den except when it's sunny outside. This might be a way of avoiding conditions that let a predator sneak up and pounce. The squirrels reside in a wide variety of environments, adapting their burrow networks to each, and eat a wide variety of food, including lots of insects, seeds and grasses, but also extending to small mice or young chickens. They occur in all three parks, typically in shady spots where trees offer them refuge. The Rankin Ridge region of Wind Cave National Park is a good spot to find them.

## LEAST CHIPMUNK

The least chipmunk *(Eutamias minimus)* gets its name because it is the least—the smallest—of all chipmunks. It is also the lightest in color. But it is one of the most in numbers, making it easy to see in many places within the three national parks.

Dark lines run across its face and down its back; the least chipmunk holds its dark and furry tail nearly straight up as it bounces across the ground like a rubber ball with legs. They live mostly in sagebrush flats, particularly in the scattered brush of Theodore Roosevelt National Park's South Unit, but may take advantage of nearby trees, even nesting high among the branches if they have the opportunity. Even if the chipmunk is hidden above, you can tell whether it is around by listening for its high-pitched chirping. They mostly prefer acorns, nuts and other vegetable matter that they stuff into their cheeks and carry to a kind of chipmunk lunchroom—a stump or log where they can maintain a vigilant watch for predators.

Like all chipmunks, the least chipmunk has large front teeth that grow continuously and are whittled down only by the grinding against each other that takes place whenever the chipmunk munches a snack.

## SHARP-TAILED GROUSE

If it's spring courtship time for the sharp-tailed grouse (*Tympanuchus phasianellus*) and you come across some of these showy birds, the males are sure to catch your attention. In fact, they are trying to catch attention—the attention of female grouse. To do so, they puff up their chests, spread their wings and tails, drop their heads, blow up a purplish air sac on their throats and stomp the ground creating a sort of drumming sound while they bow and preen. Vibrating wing quills add a faint rattle. It's reasonable to ask: How could the females possibly ignore their male counterparts as they strut their stuff?

The sharp-tailed grouse can be distinguished from other grouse, some of which are called prairie chickens, by its buffy-white, knife-like tail sticking up behind it. The birds prefer open grasslands, nibbling on seeds, leaves, grass and insects. They have not been dissuaded by the kind of tree-clearing that has left other prairie birds short on nesting habitat and are visible in all three parks. Look for them along the sparsely traveled roads in the eastern half of Wind Cave National Park and near the Bentonitic Clay Overlook in the North Unit of Theodore Roosevelt National Park.

## KILLDEER

Both the killdeer's scientific *(Charadrius vociferus)* and its non-scientific name describe this shorebird well. It is indeed vociferous, as its Latin name implies, repeating a *"kill-DEER"* call so often that it sounds like a broken record.

The robin-sized bird related to the seaside plover has brown wings, a downy white underside and two bold, black rings around its neck and breast. In flight, a white stripe runs across the trailing edge of its wings almost to the tips. The killdeer is at home on the coast, and usually retreats to the East and West Coasts during the winter, but it spends much of the warmer part of the year in the Great Plains and north to Canada. The species visits all three parks, often lingering amid dense grasslands. The birds nest in depressions lined with smooth stones and grasses and have developed a seemingly risky but effective way of protecting their nestlings.

When a predator approaches its nest, the adult bird drags one of its wings and limps across the ground as if the wing were broken, leading a predator looking for an easy meal away from the nest. When the predator finally gets close, the killdeer flies off, crying its telltale call to warn its cohorts.

## WESTERN KINGBIRD

Very territorial, the eastern kingbird *(Tyrannus verticalis)* belongs to a family of birds known as the tyrant flycatchers. And, in their element, the kingbirds are indeed tyrant kings. They are fiercely independent, attacking and driving off birds even as big as crows, more than twice their size.

Kingbirds are prominent on the plains; their dark heads and wings contrast with their yellowish undersides, topped off by a red patch on the crown. Their tails are black lined with white. They are noisy, with a call that sounds like a squeaky door combined with a drum roll. When airborne, the kingbird is an acrobat, snatching berries off branches and, during courtship, tumbling down through the air, recovering and zig-zagging off, squeaking all the while. Both the western kingbird and its sister species, the eastern kingbird, are champion migrators, nesting on the Great Plains and as far north as subarctic Canada, but whiling away the winter in the lush jungles of Central and South America. They are visible throughout the habitats of all three parks.

## CLIFF SWALLOW

Cliff swallows *(Hirundo pyrrhonota)* are admirable and ambitious architects. They build their mud nests in great colonies in the crevices of sheer cliffs, or the overhangs of bridges or buildings, plastering the mud into a jug-like, enclosed chamber the size of a large gourd, with an entrance hole on the exposed side. They are common in Badlands, but occur in all three parks, often blending into the chalky earth. Inside, these cozy cubbyholes are lined with grass and feathers. Barn swallow nests are similarly constructed, but are sturdy, open cups rather than a complete globe.

Standing beneath a swallow colony, you can hear the endless twittering of these streamlined, insect-eating birds that make a regular spring return to the continental United States after wintering in South America. Cunning cliff swallows may deposit eggs into the nests of other swallows, spreading their offspring (and genes) more widely through the local population.

The cliff swallow has a dark head, gray-blue wings and white breast. The arrival of foreign house sparrows into the United States has played havoc on swallows since the exotic intruders drive cliff swallows from their carefully crafted cliff houses.

## COMMON CROW

No other bird is quite as jet-black as the common crow (*Corvus brachyrhynchos*), so look for a bird that is entirely as black as coal. Another way to identify this bold species is by its unceasing *"caw-caw, caw-caw"*—a telltale sound that gives its owner away the moment you hear it.

Another of the crow's unusual qualities is its obvious intelligence, which drives many farmers up the wall. Crows have been known to eat some 650 different foodstuffs: insects, carrion, birds and bird eggs, frogs, snakes, snails, fruit and seeds. But the crow is especially fond of domestic crops such as corn, prompting farmers to try to deter its assaults through various means, the most obvious of which is the scarecrow. Such methods usually meet with only limited success—crows soon learn there is no reason to back off. If people do manage to scare crows off, they may be left with heavy infestations of insects the crows feed upon. Slightly smaller than the raven, the crow's intelligence has been proven by studies showing that it can count, solve puzzles and talk in crowspeak by combining its vocabulary of more than 20 different sounds.

Despite such high-flying talents, crows have a simple courtship. They construct nests that look like woven baskets (which may include such unnatural items as plastic wrappers and tinfoil) and sometimes roost in large rookeries that are home to thousands of birds. Look for them throughout all three parks.

## SANDHILL CRANE

They might look odd on the Great Plains with their long, spindly legs and long, narrow beaks that resemble the features of many shorebirds. But sandhill cranes *(Grus canadensis)* are common in the Dakotas, especially during the spring and fall when they are moving between their wintering grounds in Mexico and the southern coasts to their nesting zones to the north, near and even above the Arctic Circle. Their deep murmuring cries, generated by windpipes that wind around like a tangled rope, are the first clue they are around. If you hear the sounds, look up, where you may see the steel-blue cranes with a silhouette as graceful as an antique airplane. Like many other waterfowl, they often fly in a V-shaped formation, where they ride the ripples from each other's wings as if they were surfing in the wake of a boat.

On the ground, cranes stand three to four feet tall and favor wet bogs and river bottoms. You can identify them by their bald, reddish skullcap. They lay their eggs on the ground and the young are gangling at first and may not fly for three months. Cranes have suffered from overhunting and habitat loss, but now seem to be holding their own. The Little Missouri River in Theodore Roosevelt National Park is a good place to find their spindly forms.

## COMMON NIGHTHAWK

Common nighthawks (*Chordeiles minor*) are typically nocturnal, but the best time to spot them is at dawn or dusk as they flap through the sky grabbing insects with a noise that sounds like the brief buzzing of a kitchen timer. Scientifically they are not hawks, but they are voracious consumers of annoying bugs, so their cry, a little like the squeaky brakes of a car, should be a welcome sound, especially around campgrounds. In all three parks, search branches of large cottonwood trees for nighthawks.

Since they largely hunt at night, nighthawks roost during the long days of their summertime climes, when their speckled brown and white coloring blends with the bark of trees or golden grasses, making them nearly invisible to predators. They have an odd way of nesting: they simply do not nest. Instead, they lay their eggs on bare ground or even the flat, pebbled roofs of buildings, where the eggs may roll around a bit before they hatch. But this does not seem to affect the success of the young, since large flocks of nighthawks are common during the feeding hours.

## NORTHERN SHRIKE

Few animals use tools, but the northern shrike *(Lanius excubitor)* is among those that do. This gray, black and white bird, somewhat resembling a jay, uses its strong, hooked beak to grab smaller birds, mice and insects and then frequently impales its prey on sharp thorns or barbed wire for safekeeping. It's not much different from people who grab frozen dinners to have on hand for sustenance on a rainy day. Look for such ready-made meals on fence-lines or thorny plants while you tour the national parks. If you find any, you'll know the northern shrike is near.

Shrikes have pale gray feathers on their backs and snowy white down on their chests, with striking black lines over their eyes, and often stand out at the top of trees or fence posts while they watch for prey in the open. Since they rely on rodents as an important food source, shrike populations fluctuate widely along with the abundance of rodents within their ranges.

The female northern shrike lays her clutch of eggs in early June. The eggs hatch around mid-June and by early July, the young begin to leave the nest. By the end of July they are independent. Watch for them in the Peaceful Valley section of the South Unit of Theodore Roosevelt National Park.

# SO YOU'D LIKE TO KNOW MORE?

For more information about the national parks and wildlife covered in this book, you may write or call the parks directly. Other good information sources are the non-profit natural history associations that sell books, maps and other materials about the parks and their surroundings.

Badlands National Park
P.O. Box 6
Interior, SD  57750
(605) 433-5361

Badlands
    Natural History Association
P.O. Box 6
Interior, SD  57750
(605) 433-5489

Wind Cave National Park
RR 1, Box 190
Hot Springs, SD  57747
(605) 745-4600

Jewel Cave
    National Monument
RR 1, Box 60
Custer, SD  57730
(605) 673-2288

Custer State Park
HC 83, Box 70
Custer, SD  57730
(605) 255-4515

Black Hills Parks
    and Forests Association
RR 1, Box 190
Hot Springs, SD  57747
(605) 745-4600

Theodore Roosevelt
    National Park
P.O. Box 7
Medora, ND  58645
(701) 623-4466

Theodore Roosevelt
    Nature and History Association
P.O. Box 167
Medora, ND  58645
(701) 623-4884

# SELECTED READING LIST

To learn more about the national parks and wildlife covered in this book, turn to the following sources:

*The Audubon Illustrated Handbook of American Birds*, by Edgar M. Reilly, Jr.

*The Audubon Society Field Guide to North American Mammals*, by John O. Whitaker, Jr.

*The Audubon Society Nature Guides: Forests*, by Stephen Whitney

*The Audubon Society Nature Guides: Grasslands*, by Lauren Brown

*Badlands: Its Life and Landscape*, by Joy Keve Hauk

*An Introduction to Custer State Park*, by Jerry Sanders and Tom Baskett, Jr.

*It's a Dog's Life* [prairie dogs], by the Theodore Roosevelt Nature and History Association

*Mammals of the Intermountain West*, by Samuel I. Zeveloff

*North Dakota Wildlife Viewing Guide*, by Joseph Knue

*Our Living Resources: A Report to the Nation on the Distribution, Abundance and Health of U.S. Plants, Animals and Ecosystems*, by the National Biological Service

*Painted Canyon: A Window to Theodore Roosevelt National Park*, by the Theodore Roosevelt Nature and History Association

*Theodore Roosevelt National Park: The Story Behind the Scenery*, by Henry A. Schoch and Bruce M. Kaye

*This Curious Country: Badlands National Park*, by Mary Durant and Michael Harwood

*Under Wing and Sky: Birds of the Badlands and the Black Hills*, by Michael M. Melius

*The Wild Ones: An Introduction to the Horses in Theodore Roosevelt National Park*, by Castle McLaughlin

*Wildlife in America*, by Peter Matthiessen

*Wind Cave Handbook*, by the National Park Service